Eighteenth Century English Æsthetics

A Bibliography

by

John W. Draper

1968
OCTAGON BOOKS, INC.
New York

Originally published in 1931

Reprinted 1968
by special arrangement with John W. Draper
OCTAGON BOOKS, INC.
175 Fifth Avenue
New York, N. Y. 10010

Library of Congress Catalog Card Number: 68-16769

Printed in U.S.A. by
NOBLE OFFSET PRINTERS, INC.
NEW YORK 3, N. Y.

PREFACE.

To the making of books there is no end; and thus bibliographies have their use, albeit a humble one. Unhappily, however, this very text that enjoins the value of such works points out the hopelessness of their success; for, if the making of books be infinite, how perfect then are bibliographies, composed as they are within the confines of space and time; and furthermore, what of the poor, finite compilers of such things? But even if the compiler be meticulously exact and unflinchingly exhaustive and so produce a sort of masterpiece, he is a mere servant in the intellectual life, and his work a mere convenience to the hand of the historians, critics and scientists on whom its right of existence depends. Occasionally, however, the bibliographer has a wider function in that he can bring to light an aspect of human endeavor that history has not chronicled, and call the attention of his betters to a territory that they have not explored.

The general neglect of eighteenth century æsthetic theory, at least until very recent years, has occasioned remark both in Germany and in England[1]; and, indeed, until a short time ago, the subject was not only ignored but almost utterly unknown: in 1865, Milsand referred to Ruskin as if he were the first English writer on æsthetics[2]; a few years later, Schasler noted only Shaftesbury, Burke, Hogarth, and Lord Kames, and sum-

---

[1] J. G. Robertson, *Mod. Lang. Rev.*, XXI, 108—109.

[2] J. Milsand, *L'Esthétique anglaise, étude sur M. John Ruskin*, Paris, 1864.

marized the general trend in a few phrases that might
well be examined before they are approved[3]; and von
Stein added to this list only Hutcheson, Harris, Webb,
Young and a few besides.[4] Gayley and Scott's bibliography[5] gives very little on English æsthetics of the
eighteenth century; and even Sir Leslie Stephen, who
shared with Lecky the primacy of scholarship on the
period, declared that "English speculation on such matters was nearly a blank."[6] Walker went so far as to
remark that "until the nineteenth century, they [the fine
arts] never had in England a literature of their own."[7]
Bosanquet ruled out Lord Kames, Burke and others as
"critics" rather than philosophers[8], and in his bibliography gave scarsely half a dozen English titles from
the period. He implied, moreover, that English æsthetics
took its rise only about two hundred years ago, and
referred to "the intermission of æsthetic philosophy,
from the time of Plotinus to the eighteenth century of
our own era."[9] Such a statement postulates either a
very narrow definition of æsthetics or an ignorance of
the Mediæval discussions of rhetoric and of artistic
theory[10]—not to mention the omission of such Renais-
sance works as Boccaccio's *De Genealogiis*, the poetic

[3] M. Schasler, *Kritische Geschichte der Ästhetik*, Berlin, 1872.
[4] K. H. von Stein, *Die Entstehung der Neueren Ästhetik*, Stuttgart, 1886.
[5] C. M. Gayley and F. N. Scott, *A Guide to the Literature of
Æsthetics*, Berkeley, Cal., 1890.
[6] L. Stephen, *Studies of a Biographer*, New York, 1907, III, 81.
[7] Hugh Walker, *The Literature of the Victorian Era*, Cambridge
[England], 1910, 983.
[8] B. Bosanquet, *History of Æsthetics*, New York, 1917, 171.
[9] *Ibid.*, 167.
[10] See H. V. Routh, *God, Man and Epic Poetry*, Cambridge
[England], 1927; M. W. Bundy, *The Theory of Imagination in Classical and Mediæval Thought*, Urbana [Ill.], 1927; E. Faral, *Les Arts
poétiques du XIIe et du XIIIe Siècle*, Paris, 1923; and C. S. Baldwin,
Mediæval Rhetoric and Poetic, New York, 1928.

treatises of Castelvetro, Minturno, Vida and their con-
temporaries and the twentieth of Tasso's *Dialogues*. Croce
echoes the same point of view, and points to Giambattista Vico as having discovered the new science in the
1740's.[11] Bergmann starts his *Geschichte der Ästhetik*
"gegen Ende des 18. Jahrhunderts"[12], and apparently
does not even deem it necessary to include Baumgarten
whose *Æsthetica* gave currency to the study's modern
name. Folkierski omits Pope, Young, Johnson, Reynolds
and many others.[13] Indeed, only recently, Mirabent y
Vilaplana[14], although his whole volume is devoted to
English æsthetics of the century, mentions only "los
analiticos", Addison, Hogarth, Burke, Lord Kames and
Reynolds, and "los intuicionistas", Shaftesbury and Hutcheson, and in an appendix adds Gerard, Alison, Hume
and Reid. The scope of the present bibliography is suf-
ficient commentary on such abbreviated surveys.[15]

The definition of æsthetics is, to be sure, peculiarly
elusive; and this fact may in some cases explain the
omissions of former historians; and this elusiveness of
definition has certainly been a constant stumbling block

----

[11] B. Croce, *The Philosophy of Giambattista Vico*, tr. Collingwood, New York, 1913, 46—47.

[12] E. Bergmann, *Geschichte der Ästhetik*, Leipzig, 1914, 5.

[13] W. Folkierski, *Entre le classicisme*, Paris, 1925.

[14] Francisco Mirabent y Vilaplana, *La Estetica Inglesa del Siglo
XVIII*, Collection Socrates, II, Barcelona, 1927.

[15] The eighteenth century, especially its latter decades, teemed
with discussion of artistic theories: even in England, it was an age
of theories; and the cultivation of the fine arts and an effort to
find an easy road to culture, seem especially to have engaged the
attention of the rising bourgeoisie. The reviewers reflect this urge
by occasionally noting the "numerous" writers on music or some
other art (*Critical Review*, XXXI, 458) or by lamenting the lack of
some desired treatise (*Monthly Review*, LXXV, 105; VI N. S., 196).
At the end of the century one hears a note of doubt and disillusion
(R. Burrowes, *Trans. of the Royal Irish Academy*, Dublin, 1797, Polite
Literature, 71).

to the present compiler. A great number of items, the
titles of which seemed on first sight to demand inclusion,
proved quite otherwise upon examination: Brooke's *Universal Beauty*[16] is metaphysical rather than æsthetic; *Of
Beauty* and Dr. Cosens's *Economy of Beauty*[17] and sundry
like pieces, turned out to be mere rhapsodies on female
charms; and J. B.'s *Art of Beauty*[18] introduces an advertisement of cosmetics[19]; Bedford's *Excellency of Divine
Music*[20] is a sermon on I Corinthians, xiv, 15; Grierson's
Art of Painting[21] is a mere broadside; and *Every Man
his own Gardiner*[22]; together with many other titles of
the sort, refers merely to a practical *vade mecum* that
does not even boast an introduction or a preface on
æsthetic theory. Titles then are deceptive; but, even
when the contents of the books are known, the proper
definition of the field is so difficult that many doubtful
cases of inclusion must arise. In general, the compiler,
in adjudicating such cases, has tried to adhere to the
following principles. General art-theory and the theory
of special arts should be put in, but not histories, bio-
graphies, or the legion criticisms of single works, unless
they contain conspicuous and notable discussions of some
æsthetic problem or of some art or *genre:* thus Johnson's
Lives of the Poets is included only for the sake of a
few scattered paragraphs. Text-books, especially those on
rhetoric, that are written in a more liberal, philosophic

---

[16] *Of Beauty, To the Earl of . . .* London, 1757. (See *Monthly
Review,* XVI, 460.)

[17] [John] Cosens, *The Economy of Beauty,* London, 1777. (See
Critical Review, XXXIV, 372.)

[18] J. B., *The Art of Beauty,* London, 1719.

[19] Aubrey Beardsley to the contrary notwithstanding, the present
writer declines to include this type of painting among the *beaux arts.*

[20] The Rev. Arthur Bedford, *The Excellency of Divine Musick,*
London, 1733.

[21] [? C. Grierson], *The Art of Printing,* Dublin, 1764.

[22] J. Mawe [John Abercrombie], *Every Man his own Gardiner,*
London, 1767.

vein, may well appear; but those that comprise a mere list of rules and errors scarcely seem germane. The periodical essays of the century are listed under the periodical's title, with a cross - reference under the author's name if it is known; but newspapers and magazines are generally omitted; and such reviews as chance to be included are regularly appended to the entry of the book they comment on. Greek and Latin treatises in print in England, and contemporary foreign works translated into English, or at least having some English fame, are regularly listed under the author; and the editor's or translator's comment, if significant, appears at least in a cross-reference; but in the present chaos of the field, the question of foreign influence is sometimes mere guess work. Indeed, all these distinctions are as difficult to apply as they are necessary; and there is sure to be difference of opinion.

For the convenience of scholars whose interests embrace a narrow scope, the items thus selected have been grouped alphabetically under the several arts or under the heading of general æsthetics; and, in an appendix have been added some recent discussions of the period. A considerable effort has been made to find the first edition, or the first during the century, of each listed work; the existence of later editions is only incidentally noted; and, in distinguishing editions, the writer has found indeed that "it is seldom practicable to go behind the actual titlepages."[23] The object of the bibliography is to inform scholars of the existence of material rather than to distinguish valuable editions for collectors; and consequently some expense has been saved by giving the titles only in a shortened form; and only a casual effort has been made at collating the contents. The leading subjects and chapter-headings, however, of

---

[23] R. W. Chapman, *Rev. of Eng. Stud.*, III, 77.

8 Preface.

many of the items are listed as an aid to rapid reference, especially in the case of rarer works; and the
references to contemporay reviews are useful as evid-
ence of popularity.

The compiler takes pleasure in thanking the John
Simon Guggenheim Foundation for subsidizing the neces-
sary researches in England, and owes acknowledgments
to the custodians of Harvard University Library, the
Boston Public Library, the New York Public Library, the
Library of the University of Iowa, the Library of the
University of Minnesota, the Library of the University
of Maine, the Bodleian Library, and the British Museum.
To Professor J. Hoops of the University of Heidelberg
for arranging publication in this series and to West
Virginia University for helping to make it possible,
thanks are due. For the suggestion, moreover, of items
that might otherwise have escaped his notice, he wishes
to express his thanks to S. H. Monk Esq. lately of Princeton University, to his colleague, M. W. Kelley Esq.,
to Mrs. P. Reed of West Virginia University, and especially to his wife for many days spent among the dusty
files of old periodicals. The labor has been long; for,
indeed, to the making of books, there is no end.

J. W. D.

West Virginia University
May 1, 1930.

CONTENTS.

PART I.
GENERAL WORKS ON ÆSTHETICS.

Acier, A. d': La poétique d'Aristote... Amsterdam, 1692.

Notes by d'Acier. Tr. into English, London, 1705.

Addison, Joseph: See Spectator, Tatler and Freeholder.

Adventurer, The: II, 1753, 337, 373. In what arts the ancients excel the moderns.

Ästhetische Gespräche: See Kausch, J. J.

Aikin, John: Letters from a father to his son on various topics . . . London, 1796.

Written 1792—93; vol. II, 1800. See especially I, Letters viii and ix, *On nature and art and the love of novelty;* and vol. II, Letter xvii, *On the comparative value of different studies.* See *Monthly review* XIV N. S., 1. 4th ed. 1803—1806.

Akenside, Mark: The pleasures of the imagination a poem in three books . . . London, 1744.

The order of the three issues of this edition is discussed by Ilo A. Williams, *Seven XVIIIth century bibliographies,* London, 1924, 88—99. See *Monthly review* XLVII, 429. Also ed. 1795 with a *Critical essay* by Mrs. Barbauld. See *Monthly review* XIX N. S., 26. See also Arbuckle, J.

Alembert, Jean le Rond d': Reflections on the use and abuse of philosophy in matters that are properly relative to taste. In Miscellaneous pieces, London, 1764, 177—197; and in A. Girard, Essay on Taste, Edinburgh, 1764, 219—244.

First read before the French Academy in March, 1757. See also Terrason, Abbé.

Alison, Archibald: Essays on the nature and principles of taste . . . Edinburgh . . . 1790.

See especially the essay on sublimity and beauty in the imagination and in the material world. See *Mothly review* III N. S.,
361 and IV N. S., 8. Later eds., 1811, 1815, etc.

André, Père: See Isle André, Yves Marie de l'.

Annual Register, The: 1774, 166. A new critical examination of the word *thought*, as applied to the fine
arts with rules for judging the beauties of painting,
music and poetry.

Anthologia Hibernica: I N. S., 1793, 248 and 334. History
of the fine arts in Ireland.

Arbuckle, James: A collection of letters and essays . . .
lately published in the Dublin Journal... London...
1729.

See especially No. xi on Addison's *Pleasures of the imagination*,
and No. xii on laughter.

Aristotle: Poetics: translated with Mr. D'Acier's notes
from the French . . . London . . . 1705; another ed.,
1775, without notes; tr. Pye, 1788, and again 1792
with the addition of a commentary; tr. Twining,
1789 with two dissertations, later eds. 1812 and
1851.

For Twining tr., see *Monthly review* IV N. S., 383; VII N. S.,
121; XI N. S., 241. On Pye tr., see *Monthy review* XVIII N. S.,
121. For Tywhitt ed. in Greek and Lat., see *Monthly review*
XVII N. S., 322, 368. On Aristotle, see also Batteaux, C., Moor,
James, etc.

Armstrong, John: Remarks on poetry. In Juvenile poems,
London, 1789.

See *Monthly review* IV N. S., 91.

[Armstrong, John]: Launcelot Temple pseud.: Sketches
. . . London, 1758.

See also in his *Miscellanies*, II, London, 1770. See especially
essays on language, taste, imitation etc.

Attic Miscellany, The: I, 1789, 13, On independent
genius; I, 107, Tribute to genius; II, 1790, 211,
Observations on wit.

Baillie [John]: An essay on the sublime . . . London . . .
    1747.

Barbauld, Mrs., See Akenside, Mark.

Barrett, Rev. B.: Pretensions to a final analysis of the
    nature and origin of sublimity, style, beauty, genius
    and taste, with an appendix, explaining the causes
    of the pleasure which is derived from tragedy.
    London, 1812.

Barry, James: Real and imaginary obstructions to the
    acquisition of the arts in England . . . London, 1775.

    See *Critical review* XXXIX, 91, and *Monthly review* LII, 300.
    and *Annual register*, 1775, 168. Reprinted in *Works*, II, 167.

Baumgarten, Alexander Gottlieb: Aesthetica . . . Franc-
    fort, 1750.

Bayly, Anselm: The alliance of music, poetry and ora-
    tory . . . London . . . 1789.

    See especially the *Introduction*.

Beattie, James: Essays on poetry and music, as they
    affect the mind . . . Edinburgh, 1776.

    See especially an appended essay on laughter and ludicrous
    composition, p. 321. See *Monthly review* LVI, 408; LVII, 27.
    107.

Beattie, James: Dissertations moral and critical . . .
    London, 1783.

    See especially On memory and imagination and Illustrations on
    sublimity. See *Monthly review* LXIX, 30. Ed. Dublin, 1783.

Beaumont, Sir Harry, pseud.: See Spence, Joseph.

[Belsham, William]: Essays philosophical, historical, and
    literary . . . London, 1789.

    See especially essay on genius. See *Monthly review* II N. S., 7.
    2nd ed. enlarged, 1799.

Berkeley, Bishop George: See Guardian, The.

Bielfeld, Jacques Frédéric, Baron de: The elements of
    universal erudition, containing an analytical abridge-

ment of the sciences, polite arts, and belles lettres . . . [tr W. Hooper] London . . . 1770.

Bk. II Of the polite arts in general with special chapters on
oratory, poetry, music, painting, engraving, sculpture and architecture. Bk. III, Chap. xxviii, on criticism.

Blackmore, Sir Richard: Essays upon several subjects...
London . . . 1716.

See especially the *Preface,* an *Essay upon epic poetry with a
section on the sublime,* and an *Essay upon wit.*

Blondel, J. F.: L'homme du monde éclairé par les arts...
Amsterdam . . . 1774.

[Bonnot de Condillac, Abbé Etienne]: Essai sur l'origine
des connaissances humaines ... Amsterdam ... 1756.

See especially the section on the imagination. L. Dewaule's
Condillac et la psychologie anglaise contemporaine lists the
original French ed. as 1746. Eng. tr. by Thomas Nugent, *Essay
on the origin of human knowledge,* London, 1756. See *Critical
review* II, 194.

Boswell, James: The Hypochondriack, ed. Margery Bailey,
Leland Stamford Universtiy, 1928.

See especially No. xxxv on imitation, Aug., 1780.

[Bramston, James]: The man of taste, occasion'd by an
epistle of Mr. Pope's on that subject...London...
1733.

Bromley, Robert Anthony: A philosophical and critical
history of the fine arts . . . London . . . 1793—95.

See especially Part I, Chap. ii on the superiority of painting
to writing, Chaps. iii, iv, v on types of painting, Chap vi on
the fine arts "as a source of refined polish to manners";
Part II, especially the history of patronage of the arts. For
Part I, see *Critical review* VII N. S., 377; for Part II, see
Critical review XXVI N. S., 442, and *Monthly review* XVIII
N. S., 572.

Brown, John (not "Estimate" Brown): Letters upon the
poetry and music of the Italian opera . . . Edinburgh . . . 1789.

See especially the *Advertisement* on the fine arts. Later ed., London, 1791.

Brown, William Lawrence: An essay on sensibility: a poem, in six parts . . . London, 1789.

Some æsthetic dicta in Part I on "the pleasures of sensibility". 2nd ed., 1791.

Burke, Edmund: A philosophical enquiry into the origin of our ideas of the sublime and beautiful . . . London . . . 1757.

Also eds. 1759, 1761, 8th ed., 1776; later eds. 1787, 1792, 1796 etc. and in eds. of Burke's *Works*. Ger. tr., 1773; Fr. tr. 1803; Span. tr. 1807. Also comment by F. Plumer, U. Price, A. Walker, R. P. Knight etc., and *A letter from a gentleman to his nephew at Oxford*, 1772.

Camper, Petrus: Reden voeringen van wylen Petrus Camper . . . Utrecht . . . 1792.

A sequel to the *Verhandeling*. See *Monthly review* XII N. S., 557. See also Camper's *Works*, tr. Eng., 1794. See *Monthly review*, XVIII N. S., 570.

Camper, Petrus: Verhandeling van Petrus Camper over het natuurlyk Vershilder Wezenstrekken . . . Utrecht, 1791.

Especially directed against Winkelmann. See *Monthly review* VI N. S., 206. See also Camper's *Works*, tr. Eng. 1794. See *Monthly review* XVIII N. S., 570.

Clio: or a discourse on taste. See Usher, James.

The second edition is the best.

[Cochin, Charles Nicholas]: Recueil de quelques pièces concernant les arts . . . Paris . . . 1757.

On sculpture, architecture, gardening, drama and painting.

Condillac, Abbé: See Bonnot de Condillac, Etienne.
[Cooper, John Gilbert]: Letters concerning taste . . . London . . . 1755.

On Good and Beauty, architecture, poetry, tragedy, painting etc.
3rd ed. 1757. See *Critical review* III, 421 and *Monthly review*
XI, 453.

Critical Review: VII, 434, on the exotic in art and
literature. [See also under authors reviewed.]

Dacier, A.: See Acier, A. d', and Aristotle.

Donaldson, John: The elements of beauty. Also reflections on the harmony of sensibility and reason . . .
Edinburgh . . . 1780.

See *Monthly review* LXIII, 469. 2nd ed. entitled *Principles of
taste*, containing Part III, an *Analysis of the human mind*,
reviewed in *Monthly review* LXXVIII, 259.

Drake, Nathan: Literary Hours, or sketches critical and
narrative . . . London . . . 1798.

See especially *On the government of the imagination*, and *On
the tender melancholy*. See *Critical review* XXVI N. S., 11.

[Duff, William]: Essay on original genius . . . in philosophy and the fine arts, particularly in poetry . . .
London . . . 1767.

See *Critical review* XXIII, 368.

Dyer, George: Poetics . . . London . . . 1812.

See the appended *Disquisitions*, especially Bk. I, Chap. i *On
the connection of the arts and the sciences*. Some of these
pieces came out in Dyer's *Poems*, 1792, 1801, 1802.

An enquiry concerning the principles of taste and of the
origin of our ideas of beauty . . . London . . . 1785.

See *Monthly review* III N. S., 225.

Enquiry into the causes of the extraordinary excellence
of ancient Greece in the arts . . . London, 1786.

See *Critical review* XXIV, 75.

An essay on design and beauty . . . Edinburgh . . . 1739.

A poem prefaced with a prose *Advertisement*.

Essay on original genius: See Duff, W.

Essay on perfecting the fine arts: See Newbery, J.

An essay [in verse] on the force of imagination with an ode to charity . . . London . . . 1774.

An essay on the nature and conduct of the passions and effections: See Hutcheson, F.

An essay on the use and advantages of the fine arts... New-Haven [Conn.], [? 1770].

An essay upon the sublime . . . compar'd with the French of Sieur Despreaux Boileau . . . London . . . 1698.

Essays, moral and literary: See Knox, V.

Essays, moral and philosophical: See Forbes, A.

Essays on various subjects of taste and criticism: See Macaulay, A.

Essays philosophical, historical and literary: See Belsham, W.

Essays read to a literary society at Glasgow: See Moor, J.

Estève, P.: Esprit des beaux arts . . . Paris . . . 1753.

Ferguson, Adam: Essay on the history of civil society... Edinburgh . . . 1767.

> See especially the sections on the history of the arts and of literature. Later eds. 1768, Edinburgh 1769, 1773, 1782 etc. See *Critical review* XXIII, 180.

[Forbes, A., Baron Pitsligo]: Essays, moral and philosophical . . . London . . . 1734.

> See especially the sections on the imagination, passions and books.

Formey, Jean Henri Samuel: Reflexions sur le goût. In Essai sur le beau by Y. M. de l'Isle André, Amsterdam, 1759.

Freeholder, The: No. xlv. The use and advantage of wit and humour under proper regulations. May 25, 1715. Attributed to Addison.

Freethinker, The: 1718. No. ii, on authors and the arts and sciences; Nos. cxi, cxv, cxviii, on education.

Gédoyn, Abbé: Reflexions sur le goût. In Recueil d'opuscules littéraires, Paris, 1767.

18 General Works on Æsthetics.

Gerard, A.: Essay on genius . . . London . . . 1774.

See especially the sections on imagination and on genius in the fine arts. See *Monthly review* LII, 1 and *Critical review* XXXVIII, 241 and 321.

Gerard, A.: An essay on taste . . . Edinburgh . . . 1759.

See sections on novelty, sublimity, beauty, imitation, harmony, ridicule, sensibility of taste, imagination, genius etc. See *Critical review* VII, 441 and *Monthly review* XX, 533. 2nd ed. "with corrections and additions", Edinburgh, 1764. Tr. Fr., Paris, 1765.

Gibbon, Edward: Miscellaneous works . . . London . . . 1796.

See especially II, 76, his remarks on Longinus.

Gilpin, William: See Lady's Magazine.

Godwin, William: The Enquirer . . . London . . . 1797.

See especially Part I, Essays iii and iv on genius, and Part II, xi on learning. See *Monthly review* XXIII, N. S., 291.

Goguet [Anthony Yves]: The origin of laws, arts and sciences and their progress among the most ancient nations [translated by Dunn and Speerman] . . . Edinburgh . . . 1761.

See especially the sections on gardening, architecture and sculpture. 1st ed., Paris, 1758.

Green, John: Beauty, a poem, ? London, ? 1756.

See *Critical review* I, 318, and *Monthly review* XIV, 558. I have not seen a copy. See also a satire on it entitled *The Deformity of Beauty*, noticed in the *Monthly review* XV, 90.

Guardian, The: No. xlix, May, 7, 1713, on the pleasures of the imagination, attributed to Bishop Berkeley. No. lxxxvi, on beauty in poetry, attributed to Steele.

H., J.: See Highmore, Joseph.

Hall, Samuel: An attempt to shew that a taste for the beauty of nature and the fine arts has no influence favourable to morals, in twenty essays on literary and philosophical subjects . . . Dublin . . . 1791.

Published previously in the *Memoirs of the Manchester literary and philosophical society*, I, 1785.

[Hancarville, P. F. Hugues d']: Recherches sur l'origine l'esprit et les progrès des arts de la Grèce ... London ... 1785.

Harris, James: Philosophical arrangements ... London ... 1775.

See especially Chap. XIII on position in works of art.

Harris, James: Three treatises, the first concerning art. The second concerning music and poetry ... London ... 1744.

2nd ed. 1765; 3rd, 1772, 5th, 1792. See *Monthly review* XXXVII N. S., 3.

Hemsterhuis, M. F.: Oeuvres philosophiques ... Paris ... 1792.

See especially letters on sculpture, music and poetry, on desires etc. See *Monthly review* X N. S., 531.

H[ighmore], J[oseph]: Essays, moral, religious and miscellaneous ... London ... 1766.

See especially II, 84, *Whether artists only are proper judges of works of art.*

Hoare, Prince: The artist; a collection of essays on painting, poetry, sculpture, architecture, the drama ... London, 1810.

See especially No. ii, *On originality* by Northcote; No. iv, *On the premature exercise of taste,* by Hoare; No. v, *On dramatic style,* by Cumberland; No. viii, *On instruction in design,* by Hope; No. ix, *On the independence of painting and poetry,* by Northcote.

Hogarth, William: Analysis of Beauty, written with a view of fixing the fluctuating ideas of taste ... London ... 1753.

Another ed. ? 1791.

Hume, David: Four dissertations ... London ... 1757.

See especially IV, *Of the standard of taste.* See *Monthly review* XVI, 122 *et seq.* See Sülzer, J. G.

[Hutcheson, Francis]: An essay on the nature and conduct of the passions and affections . . . London . . . 1728.

See the *Preface* and Sec. V, *A comparison of the pleasures and pains of the several senses, as to intenseness and duration.* Later eds., 1742, 1756.

[Hutcheson, Francis]: An inquiry into the original of our ideas of beauty and virtue . . . London . . . 1725.

See especially the secs. on absolute and relative beauty. 2nd ed. with alterations and additions, 1726; 3rd ed. 1729; 5th, 1753; also Glasgow, 1738; tr. Fr., 1749.

Hutcheson, Francis: Reflections upon laughter and remarks upon the Fable of the Bees [by B. Mandeville] . . . Glasgow . . . 1750.

Inquiry into the original of our ideas of beauty and virtue: See Hutcheson, F.

Introduction to the polite arts and sciences, An, including the principles of literature and the belles lettres, London . . . 1763.

The Investigator; containing the following tracts . . . London . . . 1762.

See especially *On ridicule,* with a special title page dated 1753, and *On taste.* Attributed to Allan Ramsay the Younger.

[Isle] André, [Yves Marie de l']: Discours sur les graces . . . Paris . . . 1763.

See also ed., 1763 in *Les Graces.*

I[sle] A[ndré], Y[ves] M[arie] de l': Essai sur le beau, ou l'on examine en quoi consiste précisément le beau . . . dans les ouvrages d'esprit, et dans la musique . . . Paris . . . 1741.

Also eds. 1759, 1763, 1767, and nouvelle édition, augmentée de six discours, Paris, 1770. Tr. Ger., 1753.

Jackson, William: The Four Ages; together with essays on various subjects . . . London . . . 1798.

See especially *On wit, Whether genius de born, or acquired?,*

On beauty. See *Critical review* XXII N. S., 262; and *Monthly review* XXVI N. S., 190.

[Jackson, William]: Thirty letters on various subjects... London . . . 1783.

See especially essays vii and xxiii on taste. Also eds. 1784 and 1795 with additions and corrections. See *Gentleman's magazine* LIII, 332 and *Monthly review* LXVIII, 391.

Jacob, Hildebrand: Of the sister arts...London...1734.

On the relationship of painting, poetry and music.

Works . . . London, 1735.

See 421, *How the mind is rais'd to the sublime.* Translated in *Le pour et le contre*, XIX, 1740, 183.

[Jones, Sir William]: Poems . . . London . . . 1777.

See especially Essay II, *On the arts commonly called imitative.* Also ed. Oxford, 1777.

Kant, Emanuel: Observations sur le sentiment du beau et du sublime . . . [tr. from Ger. by Peyer-Imhoff] Paris, 1796.

See *Monthly review* XXV N. S., 584.

Kershaw, Thomas: On the comparative merits of the ancients and moderns, with respect to the imitative arts, in twenty essays on literary and philosophical subjects . . . Dublin, 1791.

First published in *Memoirs of the Manchester literary and philosophical society*, 1785.

Knight, [Richard Payne]: An analytical inquiry into the principles of taste . . . London . . . 1805.

Takes up the senses in order, knowledge, imagination, judgment, the sublime and the pathetic, the ridiculous and novelty as related to literature, with some consideration of the other arts and much comment on Burke on the sublime. 2nd ed., 1805; 4th, 1808.

Knight, R. P.: See Price Uvedale.

Knox, Vicesimus: Liberal education, or a practical treatise on the methods of acquiring useful and polite learning . . . London . . . 1781.

See especially Sec. xxi on taste. See *Monthly review* LXV, 1. 4th ed., 1782; 6th ed., 1784; 9th ed., 1788.

[Knox Vicesimus]: Essays, moral and literary, London... 1778.

See especially essays on genius, taste etc. See *Monthly review* LXII, 61; LXVIII, 304. 2nd ed. enlarged, 1779; also eds., 1782, 1785, 1787, 1791, New York 1793 etc.; 16th ed., 1808.

Lady's Magazine, XI, 1780, 483, The encouragement of the arts and sciences defended; XXII, 1791, 486, On picturesque beauty, by William Gilpin.

Lady's Monthly Museum, II, 1799, 102, On taste.

A Letter from a gentleman to his nephew at Oxford [London] 1772.

Against Burke on the sublime. Attributed to F. Plumer.

Letters concerning taste: See Cooper, J. G.

Lettre de Mme. de *** à M. de ***, avec la réponse de M. de *** sur le goût ou le génie et sur l'utilité dont peuvent être les règles . . . Paris . . . 1737.

Lowth, Robert: De sacra poesi hebræorum prælectiones academicæ, Oxford . . . 1753.

See especially lectures xiv, xv, xvi and xvii on the sublime.

Lacombe [Jacques]: Le spectacle des beaux arts ou considerations touchant leur nature, leurs objets, leurs effets et leurs règles principales . . . Paris . . . 1758.

Macaroni and theatrical magazine: 1773, 545, essay on taste.

[Macaulay, Aulay]: Essays on various subjects of taste and criticism . . . London, 1780.

The man of taste: See Bramston, J.

Manchester literary and philosophical society: See Memoirs.

Manwaring, Edward: Institutes of learning taken from Aristotle, Plutarch, Longinus, Dionysius Halicar., Cicero, Quintilian, and many other writers . . . London . . . 1737.

Chiefly a treatise on education, but with some incidental comment on the theory of the arts.

Méhégan, Guillaume Alexandre de: Considerations sur les révolutions des arts . . . Paris . . . 1755.

Chiefly historical. See *Monthly review* XVI, 141.

Memoirs of the Manchester literary and philosophical society: I, 1785, 110, An essay on the pleasure which the mind receives from the exercise of its faculties, and that of taste in particular, by Charles Polier. Read, 1782. I, 223, An attempt to show that a taste for the beauties of nature and the fine arts has no influence favorable to morals, by Samuel Hall. Read, 1782. I, 405, On the comparative merit of the ancients and moderns, with respect to the imitative arts, by Thomas Kershaw. V, ii, 438, A defence of learning and the arts against some charges of Rousseau, by George Walker.

[Mendelssohn, Moses]: Philosophische Gespräche, Berlin . . . 1755.

See especially 1st and 3rd letters on beauty.

Mengs, Anton Raphael: See Sulzer, J. G.

Miller, George: See Transactions of the Royal Irish Academy.

Montesquieu, Baron de: See Secondat, Charles de.

[Moor, James]: Essays read to a literary society . . . within the college at Glasgow . . . Glasgow . . . 1759.

See especially the *Influence of philosophy upon the fine arts.* See *Critical review* IX, 177.

[Newbery, John]: Essay on perfecting the fine arts in Great Britain and Ireland . . . London, 1767.

See *Critical review* XXIII, 308.

Of beauty . . . London, 1757.

See *Monthly review* XVI, 460.

Ogilvie, John: Philosophical and critical observations on the nature, characters and various species of composition . . . London, 1774.

See especially sections on imagination, memory etc. See *Critical review* XXXVIII, 81.

On the arts commonly called imitative: See Jones, Sir William.

Percival, Thomas: Moral and literary dissertations . . . London . . . 1784.

See V, *On a taste for the fine arts;* VI, *On the alliance of natural history and philosophy with poetry.* See *Monthly review* LXXII, 177. 2nd ed. "revised and . . . enlarged", 1789.

Perrault [Charles]: Parallel des anciens et des modernes, en ce qui regarde les arts et les sciences . . . Paris . . . 1688.

Edition augmenté, Amsterdam, 1693.

Philosophical transactions of the Royal Society of London: XXIV, 227, How to judge of the age of manuscripts, the style of learned authors, printers etc. By Humfrey Wanley.

Philosophische Gespräche: See Mendelssohn, M.

Plato: Works . . . abridg'd . . . London . . . 1701.

Later eds. 1720, 1749, 1772 etc.

Plato: The Cratylus, Phædo, Parmenides and Timæus . . . translated from the Greek by Thomas Taylor . . . London . . . 1793.

Plato: The Idea of beauty . . . Edinburgh . . . 1756.

An epitome of the *Phædrus.*

Plato: Phædrus; a dialogue concerning beauty and love . . . London, 1792.

Tr. Thomas Taylor.

Plato: See Sydenham, F.

Polier, Charles de: An essay on the pleasure which the mind receives from the exercise of its faculties, and that of taste in particular. In twenty essays on literary and philosophical subjects . . . Dublin . . . 1791.

Also published in the *Memoirs of the Manchester literary and philosophical society*, V, 110.

Pownall, T[homas]: A treatise on the study of antiquities . . . London . . . 1782.

Present state of the arts in England, The, . . . London, 1755.

Prevost, Pierre: Essais de philosophie ou étude de l'esprit humain . . . Genève . . . [1805].

See especially the chapters on "sensibilité", and page 35 *et seq.* on the liberal arts and on language, and the sections on taste, music, imagination etc. The work originally appeared in the 1780's, and provoked an *Answer to the causes of pleasure of the fine arts by Prevost.* See *Monthly review* LXXXI, 1789, 595.

Price, Uvedale: A dialogue on the distinct characters of the picturesque and the beautiful in answer to the objections of Mr. Knight. Prefaced by an introductory essay on beauty with remarks on the ideas of Sir Joshua Reynolds and Mr. Burke upon that subject . . . Hereford . . . 1801.

Purshouse, A.: An essay on genius . . . Canterbury . . . 1782.

See *Monthly review* LXVIII, 275.

Pye, H[enry] J[ames]: A commentary illustrating the poetic of Aristotle. Published in the 1792 ed. of Pye's Aristotle's Poetics.

The Rambler: No. lxxviii, Dec. 15, 1750, on the power of novelty. No. cliv, Sept., 7, 1751, on the inefficacy of genius without learning. Attributed to Dr. Johnson.

Ramsay, Allan, the Younger: See Investigator, The.

Recueil de quelque pièces concernant les arts: See Cochin, C. N.

Richardson [Jonathan]: Two discourses . . . London . . . 1719.

See especially *An argument in behalf of the science of a connoisseur.* See also Richardson's *Works*, London, 1773, and the *Critical review* XXXVI, 111.

Richardson [Jonathan]: Thoughts upon thinking, or a new theory of the human mind . . . London . . . 1755.

See especially secs. III and IV. 2nd ed. "enlarged", 1773. See *Monthly review* XIV, 54.

Robertson, Thomas: An inquiry into the fine arts . . . London . . . 1784.

See especially the *Introductory discourse concerning the principle of the fine arts,* and the detailed discussion of the arts that follows. See *Monthly review* LXXIV, 191 and 245.

[Rollin, Charles]: Taste an essay [tr. from the Fr. by James Usher] . . . London . . . 1732.

Contains discussion of imagination, nature, genius, education etc.

Roscoe, William: See Annual Register.

Rouquet, [? Jean]: L'état des arts en Angleterre . . . Paris . . . 1755.

Includes painting, sculpture, architecture, oratory, music, printing, shop-decoration etc. See *Monthly review* XIII, 399.

Royal Society of London: See Philosophical transactions.

Scott, John Robert: A dissertation on the progress of the fine arts . . . London . . . 1800.

See *Monthly review* XXXII N. S., 331. Also included in *Dissertations, essays and parallels*, London, 1804, which also includes an *Essay on the influence of taste on morals.*

Seally, J.: The lady's encyclopædia; or, a concise analysis of the belles lettres, the fine arts and the sciences . . . London . . . 1788.

See especially II, containing rules for different types of poetry.

Secondat, Charles de, Baron de Montesquieu: An essay on taste. Tr. in A. Gerard, Essay on taste . . . Edinburgh . . . 1764, page 245.

Also in Montesquieu's *Works*, London and Dublin, 1777, IV, 119.

Secondat, Charles de, Baron de Montesquieu: Of the pleasures of the soul. In Works . . . London . . . 1777, IV, 121.

Treats of order, variety, symmetry, contrast, surprise, sensibility etc.

[Séran de la Tour, Abbé]: L'art de sentir et de juger en matière de goût . . . Paris . . . 1762.

Also eds., 1790 and 1796.

Sharfe, William: Dissertation on genius . . . 1755.

Shenstone, William: On taste. In Essays on men, manners and things, in Works, London . . . 1764—69, II, 311.

Sheridan, Thomas: An oration on education [2nd ed.] Dublin, 1752.

See *Monthly review* XVIII, 205.

Sheridan, Thomas: British education: or, the source of the disorders of Great Britain . . . London . . . 1756.

See especially Part III on the imitative arts. See *Monthly review* XIV, 81 and *Critical review* I, 1.

Silvain: Traité du sublime à Monsieur Despreaux . . . Paris . . . 1732.

Spectator, The: No. xlvii, April 24, 1711, on laughter. attributed to Addison. No. lii, April 30, 1711, on humor, attributed to Steele. No. ccxlix, Dec. 15, 1711, on laughter and ridicule, attributed to Addison. No. cdix, June 19, 1712, on taste in literature, attributed to Addison. Nos. cdxi-cdxxi, June 21 to July 3 inc., 1712, on the pleasures of the imagination, attributed to Addison. No. dliv, Dec., 5, 1712, on the improvement of genius, attributed to Hughes. No. dcxxvi, Nov. 29, 1714, on novelty, attributed to Grove. No. dcxxxii, Dec. 13, 1714, on the power of numbers.

Spence [Joseph]: Polymetis: or, an enquiry concerning the agreement between the works of the Roman poets and remains of the antient artists . . . London . . . 1747.

> 2nd ed. 1755, 4th ed. 1777, and several abridge eds. Tr. Ger., Vienna, 1773—76.

Steele, Sir Richard: See Spectator, and see Tatler.

Stewart, Dugald: Elements of the philosophy of the human mind . . . London, 1792.

> See especially Chap. vii on the imagiantion. See *Monthly review* X N. S., 59, 203, 366.

Sulzer, Johann Georg: Allgemeine Theorie der schönen Künste in einzeln, nach alphabetischer Ordnung der Kunstwörter auf einander folgenden, Artikeln abgehandelt . . . Leipzig, 1771—74.

> See especially *sub* Künste, Bauart etc. Tr. Eng. 1806. The items *sub* Sülzer in *Brit. Mus. Cat.* show the European influence of this critic of Hume. See also *Critical review* XXXVIII, 65, 311, 386, 464; XXXIX, 64, 237.

Sydenham, Floyer: A synopsis or general view of the works of Plato . . . London . . . 1759.

> See especially the *Io* and the greater and the lesser *Hippias*. The general title page at the beginning is dated 1767.

Taillason, J. J.: Le danger des règles dans les arts, poème . . . Paris . . . 1785.

Taste, an essay: See Rollin, C. and Usher, J.

Tatler, The: No. xliii, July 19, 1709, on the sublime, attributed to Steele. No. ccxvi, Aug. 26, 1710, on the virtuosi, attributed to Addison.

Taylor, Thomas: Concerning the beautiful, or a paraphrase translation from the Greek of Plotinus . . . London . . . 1787.

> See *Monthly review* LXXXIX, 142. See also Plato.

Temple, L.: See Armstrong, J.

Terrasson, Abbé: La philosophie applicable à tous les objets de l'esprit et de la raison, avec des réflexions de D'Alembert . . . Paris . . . 1754.

Théorie des sentimens agréables: See Vernet, J.

Thirty letters: See Jackson, W.

Thomson, Alexander: The paradise of taste . . . London . . . 1796.

See *Monthly review* XXI N. S., 274.

Thomson, William: An enquiry into the elementary principles of beauty in the works of nature and art, to which is prefixed an introductory discourse on taste . . . London [1800].

See *Monthly review* XXXIV N. S., 387.

Transactions of the royal Irish academy, Dublin, [1794], polite literature, 17, An essay on the origin and nature of our idea of the sublime by George Miller.

Read July 13, 1793.

U[sher], J[ames]: Clio: or a discourse on taste . . . the second edition with large additions . . . London . . . 1769.

See especially sections on conversation, writing, music, sculpture, novelty, genius etc. See *Critical review* XXIX, 152 and XYIII, 422. See Rollin, C.

[Vernet, J.]: Théorie des sentimens agréables . . . Genève . . . 1747.

See especially the *Preface,* and a chapter on the harmony of style. Also ed. 1750.

Villate, Cartaud de la: Essai historique et pilosophique sur le goût . . . Amsterdam, 1736.

Voltaire (F. M. Arouet): Essay on taste. In A. Gerard, Essay on taste . . . second edition; with additions to which are annexed, three dissertations on the same subject by Mons. Voltaire . . . Edinburgh . . . 1764.

Walker, George: See Memoirs of the Manchester literary and philosophical society.

Wanley, H.: See Royal Society of London.

Warburton, Bishop William: Doctrine of grace ... London, 1762.

On the sublime, in reply to Conyers Middleton's *Essay on the gift of tongues*.

Webb, F.: Poems ... Salisbury ... 1790.

See especially *Preface* and *Ode on Genius*.

Whitehead, William: An essay on ridicule ... London ... 1743.

Winkelmann [J. J.]: Essai sur l'allégorie. In De l'allégorie, ou traités sur cette matière par Winckelmann, Addison, Sulzer etc. ... Paris ... [1799].

Wotton, William: Reflections upon ancient and modern learning ... London ... 1694.

See especially the chapters on eloquence, poetry, architecture, statuary, painting, gardening and music.

PART II.
ARCHITECTURE AND GARDENING.

Aikin, J.: Letters from a father to his son on various topics . . . London, 1796—1800.

See especially vol. I, Letter xxiv, *On ruins,* and vol. II, Letter vi *On Milton's Garden of Eden as a supposed prototype of modern gardening.* 4th ed. 1803—06.

Alberti, Leon Batista: The architecture . . . in ten books . . . London, 1755.

On gardening, see Book ix. Tr. Eng. by James Leoni, from the Italian version of C. Bartoli, 1726.

Algarotti, Count: Essay on painting translated into English . . . London, 1764.

See especially the chapter on landscape and architecture. See *Critical review* XVIII, 359 and *Annual Register,* 1767, 215.

Anderson, James: Recreations in agriculture, natural history, arts and miscellaneous literature . . . London [? 1800].

See especially II. See *Monthly review* XXXVIII N. S., 398.

Anthologia hibernica, II, 1793, Architecture in Ireland.

The art of architecture, a poem in imitation of Horace's Art of poetry . . . London . . . 1742.

[Bachaumont, L. Petit de]: Essai sur la peinture, la sculpture, et l'architecture . . . [? Paris], 1751.

Beauty, a poetical essay: See Pye, H. J.

The Bee, or weekly intelligencer: II, 1791, 161, 247, 348, Remarks on Gothic architecture. V, 193, 270 and VI, 4, Cursory remarks on Grecian and Gothic architecture considered as an object of taste. X, 1792, 234, On taste in architecture.

Bentham, J.: See Warton, T.

Berthier, R. P.: Extrait de l'essai sur la peinture, la sculpture, et l'architecture . . . [?Paris] 1751.

[Bickham, George]: Stowe, the gardens of the Right Honourable Richard [Temple] Viscount Cobham. Address'd to Mr. Pope . . . London . . . 1732.

Blond, Alexander [Jean Baptiste] le: The theory and practice of gardening . . . London . . . 1712.

Also ed. London, 1728.

Bonamy: Extrait de l'essai sur la peinture, la sculpture, et l'architecture . . . [?Paris] 1751.

Bouteaux, Michel le: L'Architecture à la mode, où sont les nouveaux dessins pour la décoration des bâtiments et jardins . . . Paris [?1680].

Boyceau de la Baroudière, Jacques: Traité du jardinage, qui ensigne les ouvrages qu'il faut faire pour avoir un jardin . . . Paris . . . 1707.

Bromley, Robert Anthony: A philosophical and critical history of the fine arts, painting, sculpture and architecture . . . London, 1793—95.

For vol. I, see *Monthly review* XIII N. S., 151; *Critical review* VII N. S., 377. For vol. II, see *Critical review* XXVI N. S., 442.

Burgh, W.: Comment on Mason's English Garden: See Mason, W.

Brutis, Revis: New and accurate method of delineating all the parts of the different orders of architecture . . . [London] 1737.

Also ed. 1767.

Campbell, Colin: Vitruvius britannicus, or the British architect . . . London . . . 1717—25.

See *Introduction.*

Carter, John: The Ancient architecture of England . . . orders during the British, Roman, Saxon, and Norman æras . . . London, 1795.

See preface. New ed. by J. Britton, 1845.

Cérutti, [Joseph Antoine Joachim]: Les jardins de Betz poème, accompagné de notes . . . fait en 1785 . . . Paris . . . 1792.

Chambers, Sir William: Dissertation on Oriental gardening . . . London . . . 1772.

See especially the *Preface*. 2nd ed. with additions, 1772. See *Critical review* XXXIII, 413; *Lady's magazine*, III, 216; and W. Mason, *Heroic Epistle to Sir William Chambers*, London, 1773.

Chambers, Sir William: A treatise on civil architecture . . . London . . . 1759.

See especially *Preface*. 3rd ed. 1791.

Critical observations on the buildings and improvements of London: See Stuart, J.

Crunden, John: Convenient and ornamental architecture consisting of original designs . . . beginning with the farm house . . . London . . . 1770.

See especially the *Preface* and the bibliography of books on architecture sold by A. Webley. 2nd ed. 1797.

Cumberland, George: A poem on the landscapes of Great-Britain . . . London . . . 1793.

Dallaway, James: Anecdotes of the arts in England . . . London, 1800.

See *Monthly review* XXXIV N. S., 61.

Darwin, Erasmus: Phytologia; or the philosophy of agriculture . . . London . . . 1799.

See *Monthly review* XXXIII N. S., 113.

Darwin, Erasmus: The botanic garden . . . London, 1789.

See especially the notes. See *Monthly review* LXXX, 337. Later eds. 1791, 1794—95. Tr. Fr. 1800; tr. Port. 1803—04; tr. Ital. 1805.

Dodsley, R[obert]: Public virtue: a poem in three books.

I Agriculture, II Commerce, III Arts . . . London . . .
1753.

See especially Book II, Canto ii on gardening.

Elements of modern gardening: See Tusler, John.

Elsam, R.: See Malton, J.

Essai sur la peinture, la sculpture, et l'architecture: See
Bachaumont, L. P. de.

Essai sur l'architecture: See Langier, M. A.

An essay on architecture, on which its true principles
are explained, and invariable rules proposed for
directing the judgment . . . London . . . 1755.

An essay on design in gardening: See Mason, G.

An essay on the qualifications and duties of an architect.
. . . London, 1773.

See especially the introductory material on the definition and
divisions of architecture. See *Critical review* XXXVII, 74.

Essay upon harmony as it relates chiefly to situation
and building: See Morris, R.

Essays, moral and literary: See Knox, V.

Falconer, William: Thoughts on style and taste in gardening among the ancients, in twenty essays on literary
and philosophical subjects . . . Dublin . . . 1791.

First published in *Memoirs of the Manchester literary and
philosophical society*, 1785.

Fielding, Henry: The history of Tom Jones . . . London
. . . 1709.

See especially Bk. I, Chap. iv on gardening.

Fontanes, Louis de: Le verger, poëme . . . Paris . . . 1788.

Fréard de Cambray, Roland: A parallel of ancient architecture with modern . . . with Leon Batista Alberti's
Treatise of statues . . . London, 1664.

Tr. John Evelyn. See especially the *Preface.* Also ed. 1733.

Fre'ron: Extrait de l'essai sur la peinture, la sculpture,
et l'architecture . . . [? Paris] 1751.

Gibbs, James: Book of architecture ... London, 1728.
2nd ed. 1739.

Girardin, René Louis de: An essay on landscape; or, the means of improving and embellishing the country round our habitations, translated from the French... London ... 1783.

Goldsmith, Oliver: See The bee.

The Guardian: No. clxxiii, Sept. 29, 1713, On the laying out of gardens, attributed to Pope.

Gwynn, John: An essay on design: including proposals for erecting a public academy ... London ... 1749.

On painting, architecture and sculpture. See *Monthly review* I, 81, 161.

Hall, Sir James: Essay on the origin and principles of Gothic architecture ... from the Transactions of the Royal society of Edinburgh, IV ... Edinburgh, 1797.

See *Monthly review* XXXI, N. S., 13. Also London ed. 1813.

Heely, Joseph: Letters on the beauties of Hagley, Envil and the Leasowes with critical remarks: and observations on the modern taste in gardening ... London ... 1777.

Jackson, William: The four ages; together with essays on various subjects ... London ... 1798.

See *Of Gothic architecture*, 95. See *Critical review* XXII N. S., 262, and *Monthly review* XXVI N. S., 190.

Knight, Richard Payne: The Landscape, a didactic poem in three books addressed to Uvedale Price Esq. ... London ... 1794.

2nd ed. 1795. See also Matthews, John, and Marshall, W. See *Monthly review* XIV N. S., 78.

[Knox, Vicesimus]: Essays moral and literary, London... 1778.

See especially I, xxxvii on architecture. 2nd ed. enlarged, 1779.

Lady's magazine: XII, 1781, 399, Milton's idea of gardening, from Walpole's Anecdotes of painting. XX,
1789, 573, Thoughts on modern gardening.

Langley, Batty: New principles of gardening; or, the
laying out and planting of pastures, groves, wilder-
nesses, labyrinths, avenues, parks etc. ... London ...
1728.

Also on architecture. Later ed. 1756.

[Laugier, Marc Antoine]: Essai sur l'architecture. Paris
. . . 1753.

Later ed. 1755. See *Monthly review* XIII, 304.

Laurence, John: The clergy-man's recreation: shewing
the pleasure and profit of the art of gardening . . .
London . . . 1714.

3rd ed. 1715; 4th 1716; 5th 1717; 6th 1726; also included in
Gardening improved, 1718.

[?Laurence, John]: Paradice [*sic*] regain'd or, the art
of gardening. A poem. London . . . 1728.

L[igne], [Charles Joseph de], P[rince]: Mon refuge: ou
satyre sur les abus des jardins modernes ... Londres
. . . 1801.

Lille, Abbé Jacques de: Les jardins . . . Paris, 1782.

See *Monthly review* LXIX, 72. Tr. 1789, 1798, 1805. See
Monthly review V N. S., 154, and XXVIII N. S., 294.

Loudon, John Claudius: Observations on ornamental plan-
tations and on landscape gardening . . . Edinburgh
. . . 1804.

For Loudon's *Encyclopædia*, 1822 etc. and the bibliography it
contains, see Appendix.

Malton, James: An essay on British cottage architecture
. . . London . . . 1798.

See the *Introduction* on the picturesque. See *Monthly review*
XXVII N. S., 305. See the reply by R. Elsam, *An essay on rural
architecture*, London, 1803.

Manchester literary and philosophical society: See
Memoirs.

[Marshall, William]: Planting and rural ornament: being
a second edition with large additions of planting
and ornamental gardening . . . London . . . 1796.

[Marshall, William]: A review of The Landscape, a
didactic poem: also of an essay on the picturesque
together with practical remarks on rural ornament
. . . London . . . 1795.

See *Monthly review* XVIII N. S., 62.

Mason, George: An essay on design in gardening . . .
London . . . 1768.

See *Critical review* XXV, 469. 2nd ed. revised, 1795. See *Critical review* XXIV N. S., 448, and *Monthly review* XX N. S., 154.

Mason, William: The English garden, Book I, London,
1772; Book II, 1777; Book III, 1779; Book IV, 1781.

See *Gentleman's magazine* XLII, 18; XLVII, 331; XLVIII, 536;
Critical review XXXIII, 171; XLIV, 312; LIII, 9; *Monthly
review* XLVI, 219; LVII, 79; LXI, 76. Also with a comment
by W. Burgh, 1783. See *Critical review* LXI, 72, and *Monthly
review* LXXIII, 390.

Massoul, Constant de: A treatise on the art of painting
and the composition of colours . . . London . . .
[? 1798].

See *Monthly review* XXIX N. S., 108.

Matthews, John: A sketch from The landscape, a didactic
poem. Addressed to R. P. Knight Esq. . . . London
. . . 1794.

The *Postscript* contains *A word to U. Price Esq.* See *Monthly
review* XVI N. S., 318.

Memoirs of the Manchester literary and philosophical
society: I, 1785, 297, Thoughts on the style and
taste of gardening among the ancients, by William
Falconer.

Also ed. Dublin, 1791.

38   Architecture and Gardening.

[Milizia, Francesco]: Dell'arte di vedere nelle belle arti del designo secondo i principii de Sulzer e di Mengs . . . Venezia, 1781.

Also eds. 1785, 1792, 1798 etc. Tr. Fr. 1798.

Milner, J.: See Warton, T.

Monier, P[ierre]: The history of painting, sculpture, architecture, graving and those who have excelled in them . . . London . . . 1699.

Fr. ed., 1698; enlarged ed., 1705.

[Morel, J. M.]: Théorie des jardins . . . Paris . . . 1776.

Morris, Robert: Essay in defence of ancient architecture . . . London, 1728.

[Morris, Robert]: An Essay upon harmony as it relates chiefly to situation and building . . . London . . . 1739.

Morris, Robert: Lectures on architecture, consisting of rules founded upon harmonick and arithmetical proportions in building . . . London . . . 1734.

See especially the *Preface* and *Lecture I.*

Morris, Robert: Rural architecture: consisting of regular designs of plans and elevations for buildings in the country in which the purity and simplicity of the art of designing are variously exemplified . . . London . . . 1750.

See *Preface* and *Introduction.*

Murphy, James: Discourse on the principles of Gothic architecture. Prefixed to Plans, elevations, sections, and views . . . London . . . 1795.

Observations on modern gardening: See Whately, T.

Pope, Alexander: An epistle to the Right Honourable Richard Earl of Burlington occasion'd by his publishing Palladio's designs . . . London . . . 1731.

For later eds., see Griffith, *Bibliography of Pope.* The piece commonly appears in Pope's *Works* as Epistle IV *Of the use of riches,* or *Of taste. A miscellany on taste,* 1732, attributed to Theobald, reprints the piece with satiric notes.

Pope, Alexander: See The guardian.
Porte [Joseph] de la: Extrait de l'essai sur la peinture, la sculpture, et l'architecture . . . [?Paris] 1751.
Price, Uvedale: An essay on the picturesque as compared with the sublime and the beautiful and on the use of studying pictures for the purpose of improving real landscape . . . London . . . 1794—1798.

Ed. with considerable additions, 1796—98. See *Monthly review* XVI N. S., 315, and XXVI N. S., 423. See Knight, R. P., Repton, H., Marshall, W. etc.

Price, Uvedale: Letter to H. Repton Esq. on the application of . . . the principles of landscape painting to landscape architecture . . . London . . . 1795.

2nd ed. Hereford, 1798.

Public Ledges, The: 1760, No. xxxi. The perfection of the Chinese in the art of gardening, ascribed to O. Goldsmith; collected in The citigen of the world.
[Pye, Henry James]: Beauty, a poetical essay . . . London . . . 1766.

See *Critical review* XXI, 591.

Rapin, René: Of gardens four books . . . London . . . 1673.

Tr. J. E[velyn the younger]. Tr. Gardiner, 1706; later eds. ? 1718, 1728, 1795.

Raynal, Abbé: Extrait de l'essai sur la peinture, la sculpture, et l'architecture . . . [?Paris] 1751.
Repton, H.: An enquiry into changes of taste in landscape gardening . . . London . . . 1806.
Repton, Humphrey: Letter to Uvedale Price Esq., London . . . 1794.

See *Monthly review* XVI N. S., 320.

Repton, H.: Observations on the theory and practice of

landscape gardening, including some remarks on
Grecian and Gothic architecture ... London ... 1803.
Repton, Humphrey: Sketches of hints on landscape
gardening ... London ... 1795.

See *Monthly review* XIX N. S., 1.

Revett, Nicholas: See Stuart, James.
Riou, S.: The Grecian orders of architecture, delineated
and explained ... also the parallels of the orders
of Palladio, Scamozzi and Vignola ... London ...
1768.

See *Critical review* XXV, 345; XXVI, 161.

Ritso, George: Kew gardent: a poem ... London, 1763.
Rousseau, J. J.: Eloisa; or a series of original letters...
translated from the French ... Dublin ... 1761.

See especially letters xxiii, xxxviii and cxxx. The original Fr.
ed. appeared as *Lettres de deux amants*, Amsterdam, 1761.

Rowland, Thomas: A general treatise of architecture ...
London ... 1732—1739.
Salmon, William: Choice experiments and observations
on building, husbandry, gardening, mechanics, paint-
ing ... London, 1723.
Shenstone, William: Unconnected thoughts on gardening.
In Works, London, 1764—1769, II, 125.

See *Annual register*, 1764, 214.

Shenstone, William: Essay on landscape and ornamental
gardening. In Essays on man, manners and things,
in Works, London, 1764—1769.
Soane, John: Sketches in architecture ... London ...
1793.

See *Monthly review* XII N. S., 396.

Spectator, The: No. cdlxxvii, Sept. 6, 1712, on gardening.
Steele, Richard (not the essayist): An Essay upon gardening ... with ... observations on the history of

gardening, and a contrast of ancient with modern taste . . . York, 1793.

Also ed. York, 1800.

Stowe: The gardens of the Right Honourable Richard Viscount Cobham: See Bickham, G.

S[tuart], J[ames] ("Athenian"): Critical observations on the buildings and improvements of London . . . London . . . 1771.

See *Critical review* XXXI, 148.

Stuart, James, and Revett, Nicholas: The antiquities of Athens measured and delineated . . . London . . . 1762.

See the *Preface*. See *Monthly review* II N. S., 316. Tr. Fr. 1767.

Switzer, Stephen: Ichnographia rustica: or, the nobleman, gentleman, and gardener's recreation . . . London, 1718.

See especially chapters on statues and other ornaments, on grass and gravel, on design in general etc. 2nd ed. 1742.

[?Tusler, John]: Elements of modern gardening: or, the art of laying out of pleasure grounds . . . London . . . [?1800].

Main headings: ground, wood, water, buildings, a garden, and a ferme ornée.

Universal Magazine, The: 1747, 378, Architecture, the four orders.

Vitruvius, Pollio Marcus: An abridgement of the architecture of Vitruvius . . . first done in French by Mons. Perrault . . . and now englished, with additions . . . London . . . 1692.

5th ed. ed. Boyer, ?1703; also ed. 1729.

Vitruvius, Pollio Marcus: The architecture . . . translated

from the original Latin by W. Newton . . . London
. . . 1771—1791.

See *Critical review* XXIII, 385 and *Monthly review* LXXXI, 492
and IX N. S., 52. Also tr. P. Smyth, 1789. See *Monthly review*
III N. S., 327.

Walpole, Horace: Anecdotes of painting in England . . .
Strawberry Hill . . . 1762—1771.

See IV, 117. See *Lady's magazine* XII, 399.

Walpole, Horace: Essay on modern gardening . . . Strawberry Hill . . . 1785.

Ward, Samuel: Essay on the different natural situations
of gardens . . . London, 1775.

Ware, Isaac: A complete body of architecture adorned
with plans and elevations . . . London . . . 1756.

See especially the *Preface*. See *Critical review* IV, 298. Also
ed. 1767.

Warton, T.: Essays on Gothic architecture by the Rev.
T. Warton, Rev. J. Bentham, Captain Grose and the
Rev. J. Milner . . . London . . . 1800.

See *Monthly review* XXXIV N. S., 88. 2nd ed. 1802. See
Monthly review XXXIX N. S., 92.

Watelet [Claude Henri]: Essai sur les jardins . . . Paris
. . . 1774.

[Whately, Thomas]: Observations on modern gardening
. . . London, 1770.

2nd ed. 1770; 3rd ed. 1771; 4th ed. 1777; 5th ed. 1793 etc.
Tr. Fr. 1771. See *Critical review* XIX, 427.

Zanotti, Francesco Maria: Tre orazioni sopra la pittura,
la scultura, e l'archittetura . . . Bologna . . . 1750.

Tr. 1767. See *Critical review* XI, 63.

PART III.
PICTORIAL AND PLASTIC ARTS.

Alberti, Leone Batista: The architecture . . . in ten books. Of painting in three books. Of statues in one book . . . London, 1755.

Of painting originally appeared, London, 1751.

Algarotti, Count: Essay on painting translated into English . . . London, 1764.

Chapters on anatomy, perspective, symmetry, coloring, drapery, imitation etc. See *Critical review* XVIII, 359, and *Annual register*, 1767, 215.

The art of drawing and painting in water colours . . . London . . . 1755.

See Chap. I. Also ed. 1770.

The art of drawing in perspective . . . to which are annexed the art of painting upon glass, and drawing in crayons . . . to which is added a method of casting amber . . . [3rd ed.] London, 1769.

4th ed. 1777; 9th ed. 1818.

The art of etching: See Spilsbury, F.

The art of painting in miniature teaching the speedy and perfect acquisition of that art without a master . . . translated from the original French . . . the fourth edition, London, 1739.

In five sections, on miniature and other types of painting, on color, buildings, flowers etc. 5th ed. 1750; 6th ed. 1752.

The artist's assistant in drawing, prespective, etching, engraving . . . containing . . . rules . . . London, 1799.
See Chap. I.

The artist's repository, and drawing magazine, exhibiting the principles of the polite arts ... 7th edition ... London ... [?1799].

See *Monthly review* XXIX N. S., 451.

Avison, Charles: Essay on musical espression ... London, 1752.

See especially the section *On the analogies between music and painting*. 2nd ed. 1753 "with alterations and large additions"; 3rd ed. 1775.

B., J.: A call to the connoisseurs; or decisions of sense with respect to the present state of painting and sculpture in England ... London ... 1761.

See *Critical review* XI, 411.

[Bachaumont, L. Petit de]: Essai sur la peinture, la sculpture, et l'architecture ... [?Paris] 1751.

Bardwell, Thomas: Practice of painting and perspective made easy ... art of painting in oil ... and a new, short and familiar account of the art of perspective ... London, 1756.

See *Monthly review* XVII, 549, and *Critical review* I, 214. Abr. ed. 1795.

Barry, James: Lectures in painting delivered at the Royal Academy. In Works, London, 1809, I, 339.

On design, composition etc.

Barry, James: A letter to the Dilettanti Society respecting ... matters essentially necessary for the improvement of public taste ... London, 1798.

See *Monthly review* XXVIII N. S., 179. 2nd ed. 1799. See also *Works*, 1809.

Barry, James: Remarks on the present state of the art of painting, in Pilkington, M., The gentleman's and connoisseur's dictionary of painters, London, 1798.

See *Monthly review* XLIII, 24, and XXV N. S., 429.

Beaumont, Sir Harry [pseud.]: See Spence, J.

Bell, Henry: An historical essay on the original of painting, wherein is exhibited, I some probabilities and
pretentions to its invention before the flood, II
its commencement again after the flood, and its
progress through several nations to the time of
Cimabue . . . London, 1728.

> Chap. I treats of painting in general, and its relation to some
> of the other fine arts. See in reply *A vindication of commerce
> and the arts*. See *Critical review* V, 352.

Berthier, R. P.: Extrait de l'essai sur la peinture, la
sculpture, et l'architecture . . . [?Paris] 1751.

Bonamy: Extrait de l'essai sur la peinture, la sculpture,
et l'architecture . . . [?Paris] 1751.

Bos, Abbé Jean Baptiste du: Critical reflections on
poetry, painting and music . . . London . . . 1748.

> Tr. Thomas Nugent; first Fr. ed., Paris, 1719; 7th Fr. ed. 1770.

Bromley, Robert Anthony: A philosophical and critical
history of the fine arts, painting, sculpture, and
architecture . . . London, 1793—1795.

> See *Monthly review* XIII N. S., 151, and *Critical review* VII
> N. S., 377, and XXVI N. S., 442.

Brown, W.: See Dolce, L.

Carter, John: Specimens of the ancient sculpture and
painting, now remaining in the kingdom, from the
earliest period to the reign of Henry the VIII . . .
London . . . 1780.

> See the *Introduction* to each part and several of the essays by
> several hands.

Caylus, Count de: See Tubières de Grimoard de Pestels
de Levis, Anne Claude Philippe, Count de Caylus.

Chelsum, James: History of the art of engraving in
mezzotinto . . . Winchester, 1780.

> See *Monthly review* LXXV, 118.

[Cooke, William]: An ode on poetry, painting, and sculpture . . . London . . . 1764.

Cooper, Thomas: See Memoirs of the Manchester literary and philosophical society.

Coypel, Antoine: Vingt discours sur la peinture . . . Paris . . . 1721.

Cozens, Alexander: Principles of beauty relative to the human head . . . London . . . 1778.

See *Monthly review* LVIII, 444.

Craig, W. M.: An essay on the study of nature in drawing landscape . . . London . . . 1793.

See *Monthly review* XV N. S., 475.

Cunberland, George: Thoughts on outline sculpture . . . London . . . 1796.

See especially *To the reader* and Sec. I. See *Critical review* XXVI N. S., 453; and *Monthly review* XXIX N. S., 451.

Dallaway, James: Anecdotes of the arts in England: . . . London . . . 1800.

See *Monthly review* XXXIV N. S., 61.

Da Vinci, Leonardo: See Vinci, Leonardo Da.

De Courtney, Osborne: See The historical magazine.

Dell'arte di vedere nelle belle arti del disegno: See Milizia, F.

Diderot [Denis]: Essais sur la peinture . . . Paris . . . [1795].

See Chapter VI. See *Monthly review* XVI N. S., 491.

Diderot, Denis: See Falconet, E.

Discourse delivered at the opening of the Royal Academy: See Reynolds, Sir J.

Discourse delivered to the students at the Royal Academy: See Reynolds, Sir J. See also West, B.

Dolce, Lodovico: Aretin, a dialogue on painting [trans-

lated from the Italian with a preface and notes by
W. Brown] . . . London, 1770.

First Ital. ed. Florence, 1557.

[Dossie, Robert] : The handmaid to the arts . . . London,
1758.

On painting, enamels, glass, china etc. See *Monthly review* XIX,
276, 348; and *Critical review* V, 211. Also ed. 1764.

Drake, Nathan: The gleaner . . . London . . . 1811.

Most of the items had appeared earlier in periodicals. See
especially No. clxvii on painting and poetry.

Dryden, John: Preface [to the transl. of Dufresnoy's De
arte graphica] with a parallel of poetry and painting . . . London, 1695.

Another ed. 1716.

Dufresnoy, Charles Alphonse: De arte graphica: the art
of painting . . . with remarks. Translated into English together with an original preface containing a
parallel betwixt painting and poetry. By Mr. Dryden
. . . London . . . 1695.

Also ed. 1716. Also tr. Wills, 1754, and tr. Mason, York, 1781
with notes by Sir Joshua Reynolds.

Dyer, George: Poetics . . . London . . . 1812.

See appended *Disquisitions,* Chapter xiv.

Elsum, John: The art of painting after the Italian
manner . . . London . . . 1703.

See especially the *Preface* and the first four chapters.

English Connoisseur, The: See Martyn, T.
Essai sur la peinture en mosaïque: See Vieil, P. le.
Essai sur la peinture, la sculpture, et l'architecture: See
Bachaumont, L. P. de.
Essay on landscape painting: See Pott, J. H.
Essay on Prints: See Gilpin, W.

An essay to facilitate the inventing of landskips ...
London ... 1776.

See *Monthly review* XX, 277.

Essays, moral and literary: See Knox, V.
Essays read to a literary society at Glasgow: See
Moor, J.
Falconet, E.: Reflexions sur la sculpture, lues dans l'aca-
démie de peinture et de sculpture ... Paris ... 1761.

Tr. W. Tooke in *Pieces written by Mons. Falconet, and Mons.
Diderot on sculpture,* London, 1777.

Ferguson, James: Art of drawing in perspective made
easy ... London ... 1775.

See especially the *Preface.* See *Monthly review* LIV, 473, and
Critical review XL, 459.

Fournier, Daniel: A treatise of the theory and practice
of perspective ... London ... 1761.

See the *Preface.* See *Critical review* XII, 481. 2nd ed. 1764.

Fréard de Chambray, Roland: An idea of the perfection
of painting ... rendered English by J. E[velyn]
Esquire ... [London] 1668.
Free Thinker: No. lxiii, October 27, 1718. Poetry and
painting.
Fre'ron: Extrait de l'essai sur la peinture, la sculpture,
et l'architecture ... [? Paris] 1751.
Fuseli, Henry [J. H. Fuessli]: Lectures on painting,
delivered at the Royal Academy, March, 1801 ...
With additional observations and notes ... London
... 1801—1820.

Also eds. 1833 and 1847. See also Winkelmann, J. J., and
Gessner, S.

The Gentleman's Magazine: XIII, 1743, 100, 153—154,
The progress of painting.

Ges[s]ner, Salomon [*sic*]: A letter on landscape painting addressed to Mr. Fuesslin ... London ... 1776.

See also his *Works* in Ger. 1762 etc. Tr. Eng. Liverpool, 1802
(I, 173).

Gillier, Louis de: Essai sur les causes de la perfection
de la sculpture antique ... London ... 1798.

See *Monthly review* XXV N. S., 515.

Gilpin, William: Essays on picturesque beauty ... London
... 1792.

See especially the appended poem on landscape painting. See
Monthly review XI N. S., 17.

G[ilpin], W[illiam]: Essay upon prints ... second edition.
London ... 1768.

See especially Chapter I on *The principles of painting considered, as far as they relate to prints*. 3rd ed. 1781; 4th ed.
1792; 5th ed. 1802.

Gilpin, William: Three essays: on picturesque beauty;
on picturesque travel; on sketching landscape ...
London ... 1792.

2nd ed., 1794; Gilpin's several volumes of *Observations* on picturesque beauty in different parts of England and Scotland are
hardly more than augmented illustration of the æsthetic theory
of his *Three Essays*. See *Monthly review* II N. S., 173.

Goldsmith, Oliver: See The public ledger.
G[rose], J[ames]: Rules for drawing caricaturas ...
London ... 1788.

See *Monthly review* LXXIX, 61. Fr. tr., 1802.

Gwynn, John: An essay on design: including proposals
for erecting a public academy ... London ... 1749.

See *Monthly review* I, 81, 161.

[Harington, Edward]: A schizzo on the genius of man
... London ... 1793.

See *Monthly review* XIII N. S., 29.

Harte, Walter: Poems on several occasions ... London ...
1727.

See *Essay on painting*. Also in A. Chalmers, *Poets*, XVI, 320.

Hayley, William: An essay on painting in two epistles
to Mr. Romney [in verse] ... third edition ...
enlarged ... London ... 1781.

Hayley, William: An essay on sculpture in a series of
epistles to John Flaxman ... London ... 1800.

See *Monthly review* XXXVI N. S., 113.

Hayley, William: Poetical epistle to an eminent painter
[Romney] ... the second edition, corrected and
enlarged, London ... 1779.

See *Monthly review* LIX, 279.

Hemsterhuis, M. F.: Œuvres philosophiques ... Paris ...
1792.

See *Monthly review* X N. S., 531.

Highmore, J[oseph]: A critical examination of those two
paintings by Rubens on the ceiling of the banquet-
inghouse at Whithall ... London ... 1756.

On the relation of architecture to perspective in mural painting.

Hill, Robert: Poems on several occasions ... London ...
1775.

See especially 284 *et seq.* *On the harmony between poetry and painting*.

Historical magazine, The: I, 1799, 307, on painting,
signed Osborne De Courtenay.

Hogarth, William: Analysis of beauty, written with a
view of fixing the fluctuating ideas of taste ...
London ... 1753.

Huber, M., and Rost, C. C. H.: Manuel des curieux et
des amateurs de l'art ... Paris ... 1797.

See introduction on painting. See *Critical review* XXII N. S.,
508.

Idler: No. lxxvi, Sept. 29, 1759, on false taste, attributed to Sir Joshua Reynolds; No. lxxix, on the grand style, attributed to Sir Joshua Reynolds; No. lxxxii, on the true idea of beauty, attributed to Joshua Reynolds.

Jackson, William: The four ages; together with essays on various subjects . . . London . . . 1798.

> See *Critical review* XXII N. S., 262, and *Monthly review* XXVI N. S., 190.

[Jackson, William]: Thirty letters on various subjects . . . London . . . 1783.

> See especially essays V and VI on painting, XX on coloring, XXI on the horizantal line in nature and in pictures. See *Monthly review* LXVIII, 391, and *Gentleman's magazine*, LIII, 332. Also eds. 1784 and 1795 with additions and corrections.

Jacob, Hildebrand: Of the sister arts . . . London . . . 1734.

Kate, Lambert Hermanson ten: The beau ideal, translated from the original French by James Christopher Le Blon . . . London . . . 1732.

Kearney, M.: See Transactions of the Royal Irish Academy.

Kirby, John Joshua: Dr. Brook Taylor's method of perspective made easy . . . Ipswich . . . 1754.

> See especially in preface and contents a running bibliography of other writers on perspective. See *Monthly review* XVIII, 66. Also eds. 1755, 1765, 1768. See in reply, Edward Noble, *Elements of linear perspective*, London, 1771. See *Critical review* XXXIII, 248.

[Knox, Vicesimus]: Essays, moral and literary, London . . . 1778.

> See I on sculpture. 2nd ed. enlarged, 1779.

Lady's Magazine: XV, 1784, 432, Effusions in favour of painting, by Jonathan Richardson; XV, 1784, 480, Conjectures on the encouragement of statuary and painting in Roman Catholic countries; XXII, 1791.

231, Paintings—with a hint to artists, by Archen-
holtz; XXVI, 1795, 331, On painting.

Lairesse, Gerard de: The art of painting . . . London . . .
1783 .

Tr. from by J. Fritsch. See *Introduction.* Also ed. 1817.

Lamotte, Charles: Essay upon poetry and painting with
relation to sacred and profane history with an appendix concerning writing and painting . . . London
. . . 1730.

Also ed. Dublin, 1742.

A letter on the nature and state of curiosity . . . London
. . . 1786.

Contains discussion of drawing, painting, statuary etc.

A letter to his excellency Count [Caylus]: See Tubières.

A letter to the members of the society for the encouragement of arts, manufactures and commerce . . .
with some cursory observations on history painting
. . . London . . . 1761.

See *Critical review* XI, 415.

The lounger: III, 1786, 34, On sculpture.

Macaroni and theatrical magazine, 1772—1773, 313, 376,
470, on painting; 361, painting and poetry compared.

Malton, Thomas: A compleat treatise on perspective . . .
on the principles of Dr. Brook Taylor . . . London
. . . 1775.

See *Monthly review* LV, 169. Also ed. 1779.

Malton, James: An essay on British cottage architecture
. . . London . . . 1798.

See *Critical review* XXV N. S., 445.

Manchester literary and philosophical society: See Memoirs.

[Martyn, Thomas]: The English connoisseur: containing

an account of whatever is curious in painting, sculpture, &c. In the palaces and seats of the nobility . . . of England . . . London 1766.

See especially the *Preface*.

Mason, William: See Dufresnoy, C. A.

Melmoth [Courtney?]: The progress of painting . . . London, 1775.

See *Critical review* XXXIX, 250.

Mémoires de l'institut national . . . Paris . . . 1798.

See especially Pierre Charles Levesque on Greek painting and Ameilhon on ancient coloring. See *Monthly review* XXXI N. S., 462.

Memoirs of the Manchester literary and philosophical society: III, 1791, 510, Observations on the art of painting among the ancients, by Thomas Cooper; V, Part II, 1798, 407, Essay on the beautiful in the human form, by George Walker.

Mengs, Sir Anthony: Sketches on the art of painting . . . translated from the original Spanish by John Talbot Dillon . . . London . . . 1782.

On styles, composition, design etc. See *Monthly review* LXVII, 393. Also tr. 1796, including his *Reflections upon beauty and taste in painting,* his notes on the sublime and graceful styles, design, coloring, invention, composition and his rules for teaching painting.

[Milizia, Francesco]: Dell'arte di vedere nelle belle arti del disegno secondo i principii di [J. G.] Sulzer e di [A. R.] Mengs . . . Venezia, 1781.

On sculpture, painting, and architecture. Eds. 1792, 1798 ect. Tr. Fr. 1798.

Monier, P[ierre]: The history of painting, sculpture, architecture, and those who have excelled in them . . . London . . . 1699.

Fr. ed. 1698; enlarged ed. 1705.

Moor, James: Essays read to a literary society . . . within
the college at Glasgow . . . Glasgow . . . 1759.

See especially *On the composition of a picture.* See *Critical review* IX, 177.

Muentz, J. H.: Encaustic: or Count Caylus's method of
painting in the manner of the ancients . . . London
. . . 1760.

See *Critical review* X, 26.

Opie, John: Lectures on painting delivered at the Royal
Academy of arts . . . London . . . 1809.

Ozell, John: See Piles, Roger de.

An Ode on poetry, painting and sculpture . . . London
. . . 1754.

Painting, a poem in four cantos . . . London . . . 1793.

Piles [Roger de]: The art of painting, and the lives
of the painters . . . done from the French of M.
de Piles, to which is added an essay toward an
English school . . . London . . . 1706.

The original in Latin and French came out in eds. 1673, 1684,
1688, 1761 etc.

Piles [Roger de]: Dialogue upon colouring, translated
from the original French . . . by Mr. [John] Ozell
. . . London . . . 1711.

Fr. original, 1699.

Piles, Roger de: Conversations sur la connaissance de la
peindre . . . Paris . . . 1708.

Piles, Roger de: Cours de peindre par principles . . .
Paris, 1708.

Eng tr., with the *Idea of painting*, 1743.

Pilkington, Matthew: Gentleman's and connoisseur's dictionary of painters [largely tr. from Fr.] . . . London
. . . 1770.

See *Preface.* See *Critical review* XXX, 355. Also ed. 1798.

A Pindaric ode on painting; addressed to Sir Joshua
Reynolds . . . London, 1768.

See *Critical review* XXV, 393.

The plain dealer: No. lx, 1734 (II, 20), poets and
painters compared.

Porte [Joseph] de la: Extrait de l'essai sur la peinture,
la sculpture, et l'architecture . . . [? Paris] 1751.

[Pott, Joseph Holden]: An essay on landscape painting
with remarks general and critical . . . London . . .
1782.

See *Monthly review* LXX, 345. Also ed. 1793.

Price, Uvedale: Dialogue on the picturesque ... London
. . . 1801.

See *Monthly review* XXXVIII N. S., 187.

Price, Uvedale: An essay on the picturesque as compared
with the sublime and the beautiful and on the use
of studying pictures for the purpose of improving
real landscape . . . London . . . 1794—1798.

Vol. I ed. with considerable additions, 1796. See *Critical
review* XXIII N. S., 42; XXIX N. S., 41.

Price, Uvedale: Letter to H. Repton Esq. on the application of . . . the principles of landscape painting
to landscape architecture . . . London . . . 1795.

2nd ed. Hereford, 1798.

The progress of painting: See Gentleman's Magazine.

The public ledger: No. xxxiv, 1760, Chinese letters, On
fashions in the arts, especially painting, attributed
to Oliver Goldsmith.

Collected as *The citizen of the world*, London, 1762.

Raynal, Abbé: Extrait de l'essai sur la peinture, la sculpture, et l'architecture . . . [? Paris] 1751.

Requeno, Vincenzo: Saggi sul ristabilimento dell'antica arte de' Greci e Romani pittori ... Parma ... 1787.

See *Monthly review* LXXVIII, 667.

[Reynolds, Sir Joshua]: A discourse, delivered at the opening of the Royal Academy, January 2, 1769 ... London . . . 1769.

[Reynolds, Sir Joshua]: A discourse delivered to the students of the Royal academy . . . December 11, 1769 . . . London . . . 1769.

See also similar *Discourses* delivered in 1770, 1771, 1772, 1774, 1776, 1778, 1780, 1782, 1784, 1786, 1788, 1790, bearing the imprint of the following year in each case. See also Reynolds' *Works*, 1797, 1820 etc. See *Annual register*, 1779, 147; and *Monthly review* XXV N. S., 28, 143.

Reynolds, Sir Joshua: See Dufresnoy, notes to Mason's tr. See also The idler, Price, U. and Warton, T.

Richardson [Jonathan]: Essay on the theory of painting . . . London . . . 1715.

Discusses invention, composition, coloring, the sublime etc. Also ed. 1725 and in his *Works*, 1773. Tr. Fr. 1728.

Richardson [Jonathan]: Two discourses . . . London . . . 1719.

See especially *An essay on the whole art of criticism as it relates to painting.* Also in *Works*, 1773. See *Critical review* XXXVI, 111.

Robinson, Pollingrove: The beauties of painting . . . London, 1782.

See *Monthly review* LXVIII, 91.

Robson, William: Grammigraphia; or the grammar of drawing . . . London . . . 1799.

See especially the earlier sections on reality and artistic appearance.

Rost, C. C. H.: See Huber, M.

Roy, C.: Essai sur la perspectif practique . . . London, 1756.

See *Monthly review* XVI, 476.

Russell, John: Elements of painting with crayons . . . London . . . 1772.

See especially the introductory sections on taste and genius. See *Critical review* XXXIV, 43.

Scott, John: An essay on painting, to a young painter. In Poetical works, London, 1782.

Also in Anderson, *British Poets*, 1794, XI, 765, and in Chalmers, *English Poets* XVII, 451.

Shenstone, William: A prefatory essay on elegy. In Works, London, 1764, I, 3.

[Spence, Joseph] Beaumont, Sir Harry [pseud.]: Crito, or a dialogue on beauty . . . London, 1752.

Chiefly on the painting of the human figure. Partial tr. Fr. 1769.

[Spilsbury, Francis]: The art of etching and aqua tinting, strictly laid down by the most approved masters . . . to which is added the most useful liquid colours . . . with a specimen of landscape and profile . . . London . . . 1794.

Steele, Sir Richard: See The tatler.

Switzer, Stephen: Ichnographia rustica: or, the nobleman, gentleman, and gardener's recreation . . . London, 1718.

See especially the chapter on statues. 2nd ed. 1742.

The tatler: No. cxxix, Feb. 4, 1710, Dutch satirical pictures, attributed to Steele.

Taylor, Brook: Linear perspective: or a new method of representing justly all manner of objects as they appear to the eye . . . London . . . 1715.

See *Critical review* IV, 199 and XXX, 385. 2nd ed. 1719; 3rd ed. revised by J. Colson, 1749. See also D. Fournier,

*Treatise of the theory and practice of perspective wherein the
principles ... laid down by Dr. Brook Taylor are ... explained
... London 1761;* and J. Kirby, *Dr. Brook Taylor's method of
perspective made easy ... London, 1754.* See also Malton, T.,
and Young, Sir William.

Thirty letters: See Jackson, W.

Transactions of the Royal Irish academy, VI, Dublin,
1797. Observations on the power of painting to
express mixed passions, by M. Kearney.

See *Monthly review* XXIX N. S., 18, and *Critical review*
XXVIII N. S., 312.

[? Trusler, John]: Elements of modern gardening: or the
art of laying out pleasure grounds, ornamenting
farms, and embellishing the views round about our
houses, London ... [? 1800].

Tubières de Grimoard de Pestels de Levis, Anne Claude
Philip de, Count de Caylus: Encaustic or method of
painting in the manner of the ancients [tr. J. H.
Münts] ... London, 1760.

See also *A letter to His Excellency Count [? Caylus] on poetry,
painting and sculpture ... London ... 1768.* See *Critical review*
XXVI, 387.

Turnbull, George: A treatise upon ancient painting ...
London ... 1740.

See especially the introductory *Epistle upon education and the
design of this essay on painting,* and the *Preface concerning
education, travelling, and the fine arts.* Also ed. 1746.

Verses on Sir Joshua Reynolds's painted window at New-
College, Oxford: See Warton, T.

Vieil [Pierre le]: L'art de la peinture sur verre et de
la vitrerie ... [Paris] 1774.

V[ieil, Pierre] le: Essai sur la peinture en mosaïque ...
Paris ... 1768.

Vinci, Leonardo Da: A treatise on painting ... London
... 1721.

Eng. tr. of *Trattato della pittura.* Also ed. 1796. See *Monthly review* XXI N. S., 346. Also tr. Rigaud, 1802. See *Monthly review* XXXVIII N. S., 397.

A vindication of commerce and the arts: See Bell, Henry.
Walpole, Horace: Anecdotes of painting in England . . .
   also a catalogue of engravers . . . and history of
   gardening . . . Strawberry Hill, 1762—1771.

See *Critical review* XVII, 113, and *Monthly review* XXVII N. S., 171. Also ed. 1782.

[Warton, Thomas]: Verses on Sir Joshua Reynolds's
   painted window at New-College, Oxford, London . . .
   1782.

See *Monthly review* LXVII, 307.

Watelet [Claude Henri]: L'art de peindre: poëme; avec
   des réflexions sur les différentes parties de la peinture . . . Paris . . . 1760.
Watelet, Claude Henri: Dictionaire des arts de peinture,
   sculpture et gravure . . . Paris . . . 1792.

See especially *Avertissement* and *sub Arts* etc.

Webb, Daniel: Inquiry into the beauties of painting . . .
   London . . . 1760.

See *Critical review* IX, 197, and *Annual register*, 1766, 225. Also eds. 1761, 1769, 1777. Tr. Ital., Venice, 1791.

[West, Benjamin]: A discourse delivered to the students
   of the Royal Academy . . . December 10, 1792 . . .
   London . . . 1793.

Winkelmann [John Joachim]: Reflections on the painting and sculpture of the Greeks: with instructions
   for the connoisseur, and an essay on grace in works
   of art. Translated from the German original . . . By
   Henry Fusseli . . . London . . . 1765.

See *Critical review* XIX, 443. Ger. orig., 1755. Also tr. 1766.
See also Camper in Part I.

Wood, John: Elements of perspective . . . with its application to architecture . . . London . . . 1799.

See especially the *Preface.*

The world: Nos. xii, xv, lix, cxvii, cxviii, and cxix, satires on the Chinese taste.

Zanotti, Francesco Maria: Tre orazioni sopra la pittura, la scultura, e l'archittetura . . . Bologna . . . 1750.

See *Critical review* XI, 63.

PART IV.
LITERATURE AND DRAMA.

N. B.: Part I, General Works on Æsthetics, should also be consulted.

[Abbott, Charles, Baron Tenterden]: An essay on the use and a buse of satire [? Oxford, ? 1786].

> Signed at the end, Charles Abbott, Oxford, June 1786. Consists of an *Introduction*, four intermediate parts on personal, political, moral and critical satire, and a *Conclusion*.

Actor, The: See Hill, John.

Addison, Joseph: See the Spectator and the Tatler.

Adelung, J. C.: Three philological essays [translated from the German by A. F. M. Willich] . . . London . . . 1798.

> Regularly appended to Willich's *Concise account* of Kant's philosophy. See *Monthly review* XXVIII N. S., 62.

Adventurer, The: I, 1752, iv, 19, Of the different kinds of narrative and why they are universally read; xvi, 91, Of instructing by fiction.

Ästhetische Gespräche: See Kausch, J. J.

Aikin, John: An essay on the application of natural history to poetry, London . . . 1777.

> See *Monthly review* LVI. 339.

Aikin, John: Essays, literary and miscellaneous . . . London . . . 1811.

> Published earlier in periodicals according to the *Advertisement*. See especially *On similies in poetry, On poetical personifications,* and *On the comparative value of different productions in the fine arts.*

Aikin, John: Letters from a father to his son on various
topics . . . London, 1796—1800.

See especially vol. I, Letter xvi, *On Pope's Essay on Criticism,*
Letter xxiii, *On the principal faults of poetical translation;*
vol. II, Letter iv, *On a criterion of perfection in writing.*
Letter xiii, *History and biography estimated,* Letter xv, *On
the advantages of a taste for poetry.* See *Monthly review* XIV
N. S., 1.

Aikin, John: See Memoirs of the Manchester literary
and philosophical society.

Akenside, Mark: Ode on lyric poetry, In Odes . . . London
. . . 1745.

Akenside, Mark: See Annual Register.

Alembert [Jean le Rond] d': Miscellaneous Pieces . . .
London . . . 1764.

See especially essays on *Translation* and *Style.*

Alembert, Jean le Rond d': Œuvres philosophiques, historiques et littéraires . . . Paris . . . 1821.

See especially vol. IV, *Observations sur l'art de traduiere,* and
vol. III, *En faveur de la prose.*

Analytical review: IV, 1789, The village curate [obser-
vations on poetry prefixed], and V, 1790, 45, 206,
479, 493, 578 for further observations on poetry.

[Andrews, Robert]: Eidyllice: or miscellaneous poems . . .
Edinburgh, 1757.

See especially the prefatory *Hint to the British poets,* on
imagery and rhyme.

Annual Register, The: 1764, 186, Remarks on simplicity
in writing; 207, Reflections on the influence of
language on opinions and of opinions on language.
Extracted from a dissertation . . . by M. Michaelis,
president of the Royal Society of Göttingen; 1765,
233, On dramatic unity, especially as observed by
Shakespeare: from Mr. Johnson's preface to his
edition of Shakespeare's plays; 1766, 194, Some

thoughts on the English Language; 1767, 221, An essay on elegies; 1771, 201, Reflections on dramatic performances; 1772, 184, An essay on the modern novel; 1795, 131, On didactic poetry; from a critical essay on Akenside's Pleasures of the Imagination, by Mrs. Barbauld; 1798, 426, Of history and poetry, from the works of Lord Dreghorn.

Arbuckle, James: A collection of letters and essays . . . lately published in the Dublin Journal . . . London . . . 1729.

> See especially No. xii on laughter, Nos. xviii and xliii on religous poetry and No. xlix on poetic ornament.

Argens, J.-B., Marquis d': Réflexions historiques et critiques sur le goût et sur les ouvrages des principaux auteurs anciens et modernes . . . Berlin . . . 1743.

Aristarchus, or the principles of composition: See Withers, Dr.

Aristotle: See Rapin, R., and Part I of this bibliography.

[Armstrong, John] Temple, Launcelot, pseud.: Sketches . . . London, 1758.

> See The versification of English tragedy, The dramatic unities etc. See also in Miscellanies II, London, 1770 and 1778.

[Armstrong, John]: Taste; an epistle to a young critic . . . London . . . 1753.

> Apparently the same work as Taste, a satire reviewed in the Monthly review VIII, 472. See also Miscellanies, London, 1770.

Art of acting, The: See Hill, Aaron.

Art of conversing, The: See Isle André, Yves Marie de l'.

Art of criticism, as exemplified in Dr. Johnson's lives, The: See Potter, Robert.

Art of dancing, The: See Jenyns, S.

Art of delivering language, The: See Cockin, William.

Art of Eloquence, The: See Polwhele, Richard.

Art of letter-writing, The, divided into two parts, the

first, containing rules and directions for writing letters on all sorts of subjects . . . the second a collection of letters . . . London, 1762.

Art of Poetry, The . . . London . . . 1741.

A poem on nature and on the subjects proper to poetry, especially satire.

Art of poetry made easy, The: See Newberry, John.

Art of poetry, The: See Newberry, John, and Fawcett, Joseph.

Art of preaching, The: See Dodsley, Robert, and see Smalridge, George.

Art of rhetoric, The: See Newberry, John.

Art of speaking in public, The: or an essay on the action of an orator; as to his pronunciation and gesture . . . second edition . . . London, 1727.

Contains a *Preface,* an *Introduction* and a *Poem in praise of eloquence.* Mainly a text-book, with æsthetic dicta *passim.*

Art of speaking, The: See Burgh, James.

Art of speaking: written in French by Messieurs Du Port Royal . . . rendred [*sic*] into English. The second edition, corrected. London . . . 1708.

See especially the appended *Discourse presenting an idea of the art of persuasion.*

Attic Miscellany, The: I, 1789, 27, The harmony of criticism; I, 57, Essay on modern language; I, 203, The actor; I, 329, Proverbs.

Baker, Henry: Original Poems . . . London . . . 1725.

See especially *Preface* on prefaces and poetry.

Barbauld, Mrs.: See Annual Register.

Baretti, G.: See Voltaire.

Barnes, Thomas: See Memoirs of the Manchester literary and philosophical society.

Bath and It's [*sic*] Environs . . . Bath, 1775.

See especially *The author to the reader,* on poetry.

Batteux, Abbé Charles: A course of the belles lettres: or the principles of literature [tr. Miller] ... London ... 1761.

The original French ed. appeared as *Les Beaux Arts*, 1746. Treats at length of poetry in general and of different types, of letterwriting, translating, oratory etc. See also II, 217—408 on drama and IV, 1—209 on oratory. See *Critical review* XI, 381.

Batteux, Abbe Charles: Principles of translation ... Edinburgh ... 1760.

Batteux, Charles: Les quatre poétiques: d'Aristote, de Horace, de Vida, de Despreaux [Boileau], avec les translations et des remarques par l'Abbé Batteaux ... Paris, 1771.

Batteux, Abbé: Traité de la construction oratoire ... Paris ... 1763.

Bayly, Anselm: The alliance of music, poetry and oratory ... London, 1789.

Also on drama. See *Monthly review* I N. S., 37.

Bayly, Anselm: Introduction to the study of languages ... London ... 1758.

See especially Part III, Dissertation iii on style and Dissertation iv on elocution. See *Critical review* VI, 372.

Bayly, Anselm: A practical treatise on singing and playing ... London ... 1771.

Contains a discussion of phonetics and an essay on "the art of just speaking".

Beattie, James: Dissertations moral and critical ... London ... 1783.

See especially *On fable and romance*. Also ed. Dublin, 1783. See also *Monthly review* LXIX, 30.

Beattie, James: Essay on poetry and music as they affect

the mind; on laughter, and ludicrous composition...
Edinburgh . . . 1776.

Also ed. Edinburgh 1778, a duplicate with a new titlepage.
See *Monthly review* LVI, 408; LVII, 27 and 107.

Beattie, James: A letter to the Rev. Hugh Blair . . .
on the improvement of psalmody in Scotland . . .
1839.

Written and printed in 1778, but not published. Contains
remarks on poetical translation.

Beauties of poetry displayed, containing observations on
the different species of poetry, and the rules of
English versification, examplified by a large collection of beautiful passages, similies and descriptions
. . . London, 1757.

The *Preface* is for the most part a cento of quotations from
Pope, Warton and others. See *Monthly review* XVI, 581.

Beckford, William: Modern novel writing; or the elegant
enthusiast . . . 1796.

Bee, The: London, 1759, 65, No. i, On the use of
language; 193, No. vii, On eloquence. Ed. O. Goldsmith.

Bee, The: or literary weekly intelligencer: I, 1790, 20,
Objections against poetry; 21, Utility of poetry;
167, Remarks on the utility of periodical performances; IV, 1791, 57, On pastoral poetry; V, 1791,
177, Letter on the essential qualities of poetical
genius.

[Belsham, William]: Essays, philosophical, historical, and
literary . . . London, 1789.

See essays on *Style, Versification, Epic Poetry,* and *Dramatic
Poetry.* 2nd ed. enlarged, 1799. See *Monthly review* II N. S.,
7, and VII N. S., 434.

[Benson, William]: Letters concerning poetical translations and Virgil's and Milton's art of verse . . .
London . . . 1739.

Berington, Rev. Joseph: Miscellaneous dissertations on the origin of plays, poetry, etc. [?London] . . . 1751.

Betson, A.: Miscellaneous dissertations . . . on the origin and antiquity of masquerades . . . London [1751].

See the *Advertisement of the reader* and *Dissertation VI* on the relation of drama and poetry. See *Monthly review* IV, 351.

Blackmore, Sir Richard: Essays upon several subjects... London . . . 1716.

Comparison between epic poetry and tragedy, 85; 189, essay upon wit; essay upon writing, 241.

Blackmore, Sir Richard: A Paraphrase of the Book of Job . . . London, 1700.

See especially the *Preface* on the stage, poetry and allegory.

Blackmore, Richard: Prince Arthur . . . London, 1695.

See especially the *Preface* on epic and allegory.

Blair, Hugh: Lectures on rhetoric and belles lettres . . . London . . . 1783.

See vol. I on literature, including lectures on taste, genius, sublimity, language, figures, style, etc.; vol. II on oratory. See *Monthly review* LXVIII, 489 etc. His *Essays* of 1793 etc. are an abridgment. 10th ed. 1806.

Blackwall, Anthony: An introduction to the classics . . . London . . . 1718.

Part I on the superiority of the ancients over the moderns; Part II on the figures of speech, etc. 2nd ed. 1719; 3rd ed. 1725; 5th ed. 1737; 6th ed. 1746.

Boileau-Despréaux, Nicholas: The art of poetry . . . made English [by Sir Wm. Soames. Since revised by John Dryden, Esq.] London, 1683.

Also ed. 1710.

Boileau, Sieur Despréaux: See Batteaux, Harte, Longinus, and Walter.

Boivin: See Longinus.

Bonnot de Condillac, Abbé Etienne: Essay on the origin of human knowledge ... London ... 1756.

Tr. by T. Nugent; French ed. 1746 and Amsterdam 1756. See especially sections on literature.

Bos, Abbé Jean Baptiste du: Critical reflections on poetry, painting and music with an inquiry into the rise and progress of the theatrical entertainment of the ancients [tr. Thomas Nugent]. London, 1748.

Apparently first published in 1719; 7th ed. in Fr., 1770.

[Boscawen, W.]: The progress of satire: an essay in verse ... London ... 1798.

See especially the *Preface*. A reply to *The pursuits of literature* by T. J. Mathias.

Boswell, James: The hypochondriack [essays collected and edited by Margery Bailey, Stanford, Cal., U.S.A., 1928].

See especially No. xxviii on criticism, Jan., 1780, and No. liii on words, Feb., 1782.

Boswell, James: Life of Samuel Johnson LL. D. ... London ... 1791.

See *Preface*, on biography.

Bouchard, M. A.: Antiquités poétiques, ou dissertations sur les poètes cycliques et sur le poèsie rhythmique ... Paris ... 1799.

Boufflers, Chevalier de: Discours sur la littérature ... Berlin ... 1798.

See *Monthly review* XXVIII N. S., 499.

British magazine: July 1761—Jan. 1763, on the study of belles lettres, attributed to O. Goldsmith.

Bromley, Robert Anthony: A philosophical and critical history of the fine arts ... London ... 1793—95.

See Part I, Chap. ii, on the superiority of painting over poetry.

Broome, William: Poems on several occasions [2nd ed.]
. . . London . . . 1739.

See the *Preface* on literary criticism.

Brown, John ["Estimate Brown"]: A dissertation on the
rise, union, power, the progressions, separations and
corruptions of poetry and music . . . London . . .
1763.

Ger. tr., 1769. Ital. tr. 1772. See *Annual register*, 1763; also
*Some observations on Dr. Brown's dissertation on the rise, union
etc. of poetry and music*, London, 1764; and *Remarks on some
observations*, London, 1764.

[Brown, John]: An essay on satire occasion'd by the
death of Mr. Pope . . . London . . . 1745.

Part I, the purpose of satire; Part II, rules for satire; Part III,
history of satire. Pope, ed. Warburton, London, 1751.

Brown, John: Essays on the characteristics [cf. Shaftes-
bury] . . . London . . . 1751.

See Essay I *On ridicule as a test for truth* and especially
Sec. iii Of the different kinds of composition; poetry, eloquence and argument. On oratory, see Essay I, Secs. iii and
iv. 5th ed. 1764.

Brown, John: History of the rise and progress of poetry
through its several species . . . Newcastle . . . 1764.

Brumoy, Père Pierre: Theâtre des grecs, contenant . . .
remarques concernant le theâtre grec . . . Paris,
1730.

Tr. Mrs. C. Lennox as *The Greek theatre*, London, 1759. The
accompanying dissertation upon Greek comedy tr. Dr. Johnson.

Buckinghamshire, Lord: See Gildon, C.

Burdon, W.: See Matthias, T. J.

[Burgh, James]: The art of speaking. Containing I. an
essay; in which are given rules for expressing
properly the principal passions and humours, which
occur in reading or public speaking; and II. lessons

taken from the antients and moderns . . . Dublin, 1763.

See especially the introductory sections. Also eds. London, 1768, 1784, and 1792.

Burnet, James [Lord Monboddo]: Origin and progress of language . . . Edinburgh . . . 1773—92.

See especially vol. III on style and Burnet's comparison of literature with other arts; vol. IV on variety, music etc. in language; vol. V, Bk. ii, *Of the didactic stile* [*sic*]; and vol. VI, on rhetoric and oratory. See *Monthly review* LXXVIII, 45; IV N. S., 369; IX N. S., 241. 2nd ed. with large additions, 1774—92; tr. German 1784—85.

Burrowes, Robert: See Transactions of the Royal Irish Academy.

Byrom, John: Epistle to a friend on the art of English poetry. In A. Chalmers, English Poets, London, 1810, XV, 213.

Byrom, John: Miscellaneous poems . . . Manchester . . . 1773.

See especially II, 21, *Enthusiasm, a poetical essay*, dated 1751.

Byrom, John: See Comberbach.

Bysshe, Edward: The art of English poetry: containing I, rules for making verses; II, a dictionary of rhymes; III, a collection of the most natural . . . thoughts . . . London . . . 1702.

See especially the *Preface* and Part I. 5th ed. 1714; 8th ed. 1737.

Calsabigi, Ramieri di: Letter on tragedy [translated with notes] by J. Penn . . . London, 1797.

Cambridge, R. O.: Scribleriad . . . London . . . 1751.

See *Preface* on the mock-epic.

Campbell, Alexander: An introduction to the history of poetry in Scotland . . . Edinburgh . . . 1798.

See especially the prefatory *Conversation on Scotish song*

between Lycidas and Alexis. See *Critical review* XXVIII N. S., 48.

Campbell, George: Philosophy of rhetoric . . . London, 1776.

Another ed. "with the author's last additions and corrections," London, 1823.

Caylas, Count: See A letter to his Excellency Count * * *.

[Chabanon, Michel Paul Guy de]: De la musique considerée elle-même et dans ses rapports avec la parole, les langues, la poésie, et le théâtre . . . Paris . . . 1785.

See *Monthly review* LXXIII, 490.

Charpentier, L.: Causes de la decadence du goût sur le théâtre . . . Paris . . . 1768.

Chastellux, François Jean de: Essai sur l'union de la poésie et de la musique . . . La Haye . . . 1765.

Circle of the sciences, The: See Newbery, J.

Clement [of Dijon]: De la tragédie pour faire suite aux lettres à Voltaire . . . Paris . . . 1784.

Cobb, Samuel: Poems on several occasions . . . to which is prefix'd a discourse on criticism and the liberty of writing . . . London, 1707.

[Cockin, William]: The art of delivering written language: or an essay on reading . . . London . . . 1775.

On accent, emphasis, modulation etc.

Cogan, T.: A philosophical treatise on the passions . . . London . . . 1800.

See especially Part I, Chap. ii. See *Monthly review* XXXIV N. S., 81 and 270.

Collins, William: Odes on several descriptive and allegoric subjects, London, 1747.

See especially p. 14 *On the poetical character*. See also later eds. of Colling, ed. Langhorne and others.

Comberbach, Roger: A dispute consisting of a preface in favour of blank verse; with an experiment of it

in an ode . . . an epistle from Dr. Byrom to Mr.
Comberbach in defence of rhyme and Mr. Comberbach's reply . . . London . . . [? 1755].

See *Monthly review* XIII, 95.

Congreve, William: A pindarique ode, humbly offer'd to
the queen, London, 1706.

See especially *A discourse upon the pindarique ode*. Other eds.
in Congreve's *Works*, 1719 etc.

Congreve, William: See Theobald, L.

Conjectures on original composition: See Young, Edward.

Considerations on the stage, and on the advantages which
arise to a nation from the encouragement of arts:
See Cooke, T.

Constable, John: Reflections upon accuracy of style . . .
London . . . 1734.

[Cooke, Thomas]: Considerations on the stage, and on
the advantages which arise to a nation from the
encouragement of arts. London . . . 1731.

Cooke, William: The Elements of dramatic criticism,
containing an analysis of the stage under the following heads, tragedy, tragi-comedy, comedy, panto-
mime and farce . . . London . . . 1775.

See *Monthly review*, April, 1775. Tr. Ger. 1777.

[Cooke, William]: An ode on beauty, to which are prefixed some observations on taste, and on the present
state of poetry in England . . . London . . . 1749.

Contains also an *Ode on taste*. See *Monthly review* II, 87.
2nd ed., London, 1756.

[Cooke, William]: An ode on poetry, painting and sculpture . . . London . . . 1754.

[Cooke, William]: Ode on the powers of eloquence . . .
London . . . 1755.

See *Public advertiser*, Feb. 7, 1755.

[Cooke, William]: An ode on the powers of poetry: to which are prefixed observations on taste, and on the present state of poetry and criticism in England... London ... 1751.

Covent-Garden Journal, The: No. X, Feb. 4, 1752, on readers and literature; and No. XXIII, Apr. 23, 1752.

Coward, W[illiam]: Licentia poetica discuss'd; or, the true test of poetry ... London ... 1709.

See especially the *Preface.*

Cowper, William: Letters, ed. Wright, IV, 18—19; Cowper to Bagot, Jan. 4, 1791.

On versification.

Creech, T.: See Horace.

Critical essays: See Greene, E. B.

Critical Review, The: XV, 161, and XVI, 1, on the nature and tendency of criticism by Edward Watkinson; XXVI N. S., 130, on biography.

See also under authors reviewed.

Cumberland, R.: See Hoare, Prince.

Curiosities of literature: See Israeli, I. D'.

Cursory remarks on tragedy: See Richardson, William.

D., W.: See Duff, William.

Dacier: See Aristotle in Part I, and see Longinus.

De la littérature et des littérateurs suivi d'un nouvel examen de la tragédie françoise: See Mercier, L. S.

De la musique considerée elle-même et dans ses rapports avec la parole, les langues, la poésie, et le théâtre: See Chabanon, M. P. G. de.

Della instituzione de' poeti: See Passeri, G. B.

Denina, Carlo: An essay on the revolutions of literature. Tr. from Italian ... by John Murdock ... London ... [1771].

A history with some introductory critical dicta. See *Critical review* XXXI, 376.

Dennis [John]: The advancement and reformation of
modern poetry . . . London . . . 1701.

On the quarrel between the ancients and moderns and the
relation of poetry to religion and morals. Also in Dennis's
Miscellaneous tracts, 1727.

Dennis, John: The comical gallant, or the amours of
Sir John Falstaff . . . to which is added a large
account of the taste in poetry, and the causes of
the degeneracy of it . . . London . . . 1702.

Dennis, John: The grounds of criticism in poetry . . .
being a preliminary to a larger work . . . to be . . .
entitled, A criticism upon our most celebrated English poets deceas'd . . . London . . . 1704.

Dennis, John: The usefulness of the stage . . . London,
1698.

An answer to Collier's *Short view*. For æsthetic dicta, see
Chap. I, *That the stage is instrumental to the happiness of
mankind*. Also in Dennis's *Miscellaneous tracts*, 1727.

Dennis, John: See Pope, A., Essay on criticism.
Discourse concerning poetical imitation: See Hurd,
Richard.
Discourse on pastoral poetry: See Warburton, William.
Discourse of pastorals: See Rapin, R.
D'Israeli, I.: See Israeli, I. D'.
Dissertation on antient tragedy, A: See Franklin, Thomas.
Dissertation on comedy in which the rise and progress
of that species of drama is particularly consider'd:
See Heppesley, J.
Dissertation on reading the classics and forming a just
style: See Felton, Henry.
[Dodsley, Robert]: The art of preaching . . . in imitation
of Horace's art of poetry. London . . . 1738 . . .

Reprinted in *Trifles*, 1745 and 1777.

Drake, Nathan: The gleaner, a series of periodical essays;

selected . . . from scarce . . . volumes . . . London
. . . 1811.

On the theory of various arts, quoted from English periodicals
of the 18th century. See especially No. 2 on critics and
criticism; No. 7 on poetry; Nos. 79 and 124 on tragedy;
Nos. 95, 101, 110 on genius; No. 105 on style; No. 134 on
satire; No. 149 on pastoral poetry; No. 174 on distinction
between and prose.

Drake, Nathan: Literary hours, or sketches critical and
narrative . . . London, 1798.

See especially the papers: *On pastoral poetry, On evening and
night scenery of the poets* etc. . . . and *On Lyric poetry*. See
Monthly review XXIX N. S., 282; *Critical review* XXVI N. S., 11.

Dreghorn, Lord: See *Annual register*.

Drummond, T.: Poems sacred to religion and virtue . . .
London . . . 1756.

See especially the *Preface* on the relation of poetry to religion
and morals. See also *Monthly review* XV, 128—135.

Dryden, J.: Albion and Albanus, an opera . . . London
. . . 1685.

See *Preface*. Also eds. 1687 and 1691.

Dryden, J.: All for love, or the world well lost . . .
London . . . 1692.

See *Preface*. Also ed. 1696.

Dryden, John: Annus mirabilis: the year of wonders
MDCLXVI, London, 1667.

See *Preface*.

Dryden, John: Defence of the epilogue; or, an essay on
the dramatic poetry of the last age. In the 2nd ed.
of Conquest of Granada. London, 1673.

Dryden, John: Discourse concerning the original and
progress of satire. In Dryden's Satires of Juvenalis,
. . . London . . . 1693.

Sometimes attributed to John Sheffield, Earl of Mulgrave.
Later eds. 1713. 1726, 1732, 1735, 1810 etc.

Dryden, John: An evening's love, or the mock astrologer
. . . London . . . 1671.

See *Preface.* Also eds. 1680 and 1691.

Dryden, John: Examen poeticum, . . . London . . . 1693.

See *Dedication.*

Dryden, John: Fables, ancient and modern, translated . . .
London . . . 1700.

See *Preface.*

Dryden, John: Of dramatick poesie . . . London [1668].

See also ed. 1733 and *Select essays*, Glasgow, 1750. See
Dryden's *A defence of an essay of dramatique poesie*, prefixed
to the 2nd ed. of his *Indian Emperour*, London, 1668. Later
eds. 1684, 1693, etc.

Dryden, John: Of heroic plays, an essay. Prefixed to
The conquest of Granada, London, 1672.

Dryden, John: Ovid's epistles translated . . . London . . .
1680.

See *Preface.*

Dryden, John: A parallel between poetry and painting.
In Dryden's tr. of Dufresnoy, De arte graphica,
London, 1695.

See also *Select essays on the belles lettres* . . . Glasgow . . . 1750.

Dryden, John: The state of innocence and fall of man;
an opera in heroique verse. With the author's
apology for heroique poetry and poetique licence
[*sic*] . . . London . . . 1677.

Also eds. 1684, 1690, 1692, etc.

Dryden, John: Sylvæ: or the second part of poetical
miscellanies . . . London . . . 1685.

See *Preface.*

Dryden, John: Troilus and Cressida, . . . London . . . 1679.

See *Preface* on tragedy. Also ed. 1695.

Dryden, John: Works of Virgil . . . translated into English verse . . . London . . . 1697.

See dedication and postscript to Æneis.

Dryden, John: Art of poetry, See Boileau, and see Dufresnoy.

D[uff?], W[illiam?]: Critical observations on the writings of the most celebrated writers and geniuses in original poetry, London, 1770.

See *Critical review* XXX, 22.

Dufresnoy, C. A.: De arte graphica . . . with remarks, translated into English, together with an original preface . . . by Mr. Dryden . . . London . . . 1695.

Ed. 1716. Also tr. Wills, 1754; and tr. Mason, York, 1781 with notes by Sir Joshua Reynolds.

Du-Gard, William: Rhetorices Elementa . . . London . . . 1673.

Also eds. 1721, 1741 etc.

Duncombe: See Horace.

Dunster, S.: See Horace.

Du théâtre ou nouvel essai sur l'art dramatique: See Mercier, L. S.

Dyer, George: Poetics; or, a series of poems, and disquisitions on poetry . . . London . . . 1812.

Some of these pieces came out in the author's *Poems,* 1792, 1801 and 1802. See especially *Preface,* and essays *On Sapphics, On Pindar's Measures,* and the appended *Disquisitions on Poetry.*

Effusions of Friendship, The: See Langhorne, J.

Elphinston, James: See Home, H.

Engel, J. J.: De Kunst der Nabootsing door Gebaarden, Haarlem, 1791.

See *Monthly review* IX N. S., 520.

English grammar with the arts of logic, rhetoric and poetry: See Steele, Richard.

Enquiry into the present state of polite learning in Europe, An: See Goldsmith, O.

Essai sur l'étude de la littérature: See Gibbon, E.

Essay on conservation: See Fielding, Henry, and Stilling-fleet, B.

Essay on criticism, An: See Pope, A.

Essay on elocution or pronunciation: See Mason, John.

Essay on English versification. In Sentimental Fables by a country curate . . . Brentford . . . 1775.

Essay on Pindaric poetry, An: Prefaced to An hymn to God . . . London . . . 1746.

Essay on ridicule, An, . . . London . . . 1753.

> Treats of ridicule in oratory and poetry. Not by W. Whitehead, though sometimes confused with his poem of that title.

Essay on satire occasioned by the death of Mr. Pope, An: See Brown, John.

Essay on satirical entertainments, to which is added, Stevens's new lecture upon heads, now delivering at the Theatre-Royal . . . the second edition . . . London . . . 1772.

Essay on the different stiles of poetry, An: See Parnell, Thomas.

Essay on the nature of English verse, An: See Robertson, Joseph.

Essay on the new species of writing founded by Mr. Fielding: with a word or two upon the modern state of criticism . . . London . . . 1751.

Essay on the power and harmony of prosaic numbers: See Mason, John.

Essay on the power of numbers and the principles of harmony in poetical compositions, An: See Mason, John.

Essay on the Pre-eminence of comic genius [on the stage] . . . London . . . 1786.

Essay on the Principles of translation: See Tytler, A. F.

Essay on the sources of the pleasures received from literary compositions: See Mangin, Edward.

Essay on the Stage, An, or the art of acting, a poem . . . Edinburgh . . . 1754.

Essay on the theatres, An, or the art of acting: in imitation of Horace's Art of poetry. In the Harleian miscellany, London, 1745, V, 543.

This piece is evidently contemporary with the *Miscellany*, and is dated by the *British Museum Catalogue*, 1744.

Essay on the use and abuse of satire, An: See Abbott, Charles, Baron Tenterden.

Essay toward fixing true stand .rds of wit, humor, raillery, satire, and ridicule, An: See Morris, C.

Essay toward the improvement of the musical art, An: . . . Glasgow . . . 1798.

Essay upon the harmony of language, An: See Milford, W.

Essay upon unnatural flights in poetry: See Granville, George.

Essays, moral and literary: See Knox, V.

Essays, moral and philosophical: See Forbes, A.

Essays, philosophical, historical and literary: See Belsham, William.

Essays poetical, moral and critical: See Newburgh, B.

Essays read to a literary society at Glasgow: See Moor, James.

Eusden, Laurence: See The guardian.

Examen Miscellaneum: See Gildon, Charles.

Examen of the new comedy, An, call'd The suspicious husband [by B. Hoadly]. With some observations upon our dramatick poetry and authors . . . London . . . 1747.

[Fawcett, Joseph]: Poems, to which is added the art of poetry, according to the latest improvements. A

poem by Sir Simon Swan, Bart., published by Joseph
Fawcett . . . London, 1798.

See *Monthly review* XXV N. S., 71; XXVIII N. S., 268.

[Felton, Henry]: A dissertation on reading the classics
and forming a just style. Written in the year 1709
. . . London . . . 1713.

Passing æsthetic dicta as in the sections on the sublime and
on taste in poetry. 3rd ed. 1718; 4th ed. 1730; 5th 1753.

Fénelon, F. de S.: Dialogues concerning eloquence in
general; and particularly, that kind which is fit for
the pulpit: by the late Archbishop of Cambray.
With his letter to the French Academy, concerning
rhetoric, poetry, history, and a comparison betwixt
the antients and the moderns. Translated from the
French and illustrated with notes and quotations by
William Stevenson, London, 1722.

Fielding, Henry: The Adventures of Joseph Andrews . . .
London . . . 1742.

See Preface, Book I, Chap. i etc. on comedy, biography and
fiction.

Fielding, Henry: The history of Tom Jones, a foundling
. . . London . . . 1749.

See especially Book I, Chap. i etc. on fiction; and Book V,
Chap. i on the three unities.

Fielding, Henry: See Covent Garden Journal, The.

[Fielding, Henry; or Stillingfleet, Benjamin]: Essay on
conversation . . . London . . . 1737.

An essay on conversation found also in Fielding's *Miscellanies*
. . . London . . . 1743. See I, 115.

Fontenelle, B. le B. de: Poésies pastorales avec un
traité sur la nature de l'eglogue . . . Paris . . . 1688.

Fontenelle, B. le B. de: Préface genérale des comédies,
Paris . . . 1751.

Fontenelle, Bernard le Bovier de: Reflexions sur la poétique . . . Paris . . . 1742.

Foote, S.: The Roman and English comedy consider'd and compar'd . . . London . . . 1747.

[Forbes, A., Baron Pitsligo]: Essays, moral and philosophical . . . London . . . 1734.

See especially the second on *Books*.

Formey [J. H. S.]: Elementary principles of belles lettres . . . tr. by Sloper Foreman, London . . . 1766.

Contains sections on taste, beauty, and art in general; on poetry and drama, and the different types of each; on prose and types of prose, including oratory, essays, romances, voyages, criticism, etc. See also ed. Glasgow, 1767. See *Critical review* XXII, 90.

Formey, Jean Henri Samuel: Mèlanges philosophiques . . . Leide . . . 1754.

See *Essai sur l'amenité dans les écrits* II, 307. See also tr. *Philosophical Miscellanies*, London, 1759.

Foster, John: Essay on the different nature of accent and quantity, with their use and application in the pronunciation of English, Latin, and French languages . . . Eton . . . 1762.

See *Critical review* XIII, 489. Also ed. 1763; 3rd ed. 1820.

Foster, John . . .: Essays in a series of letters to a friend . . . London . . . 1805.

See essays on memoirs and on the epithet romantic. 3rd ed. 1806.

[Francklin, Thomas]: A dissertation on antient tragedy. [1760.]

See especially the introductory and concluding sections. Also ed. 1768.

Francklin, Thomas: Translation of a poem . . . London . . . 1753.

Draper, Eighteenth Century English Æsthetics.

Free, John: Poems on several occasions . . . the second edition . . . London . . . 1757.

See especially the *Historical and critical account of the origin and peculiar nature of English poetry*, dated 1757.

Free Thinker, No. 63; Oct. 27, 1718. Poetry and painting.

G., F.: See Gentleman, Francis.

Gally, Henry: The moral characters of Theophrastus with an essay on character-writing . . . London, 1723.

Also ed. 1725.

Geddes, James: Essay on the composition and manner of writing of the ancients, particularly Plato . . . Glasgow . . . 1748.

See especially sections on style and kinds of composition. German tr. 1759 in the Sammlung vermischter Schriften zur Beförderung der schönen Wissenschaften.

Gédoyn, Abbé: Œuvres diverse . . . Paris . . . 1745.

See especially *Apologie des traductions.*

G[entleman], F[rancis]: Dramatic censor or critical companion, London, 1770.

Gentleman, [Robert]: An essay on reading and declamation prefixed to The new pleasing instructor . . . York . . . 1772.

Gentleman's Magazine: Vol. X, 593—596. [Dr. Johnson] An essay upon epitaphs. Reprinted in 3rd ed. of Idler, 1767, etc.

[Gibbon, E.]: Essai sur l'étude de la littérature, Londres, 1761.

See *Miscellaneous works.* London, 1796. See also eds. 1764 and 1777, the latter in French.

Gibbon, Edward: Miscellaneous works . . . London . . . 1796.

See especially II, 27, remarks on Hurd's ed. of Horace's *Art of poetry;* and on Longinus' *Treatise upon the sublime* II, 76;

and his *Essai sur l'étude de la littérature.* See *Monthly review* XXV N. S., 426.

Gibbons, Thomas: Rhetoric: or a view of its principal tropes and figures, in their origin and powers . . . London . . . 1767.

See *Critical review* XXVIII, 288.

Gildon, Charles: The complete art of poetry in six parts . . . London . . . 1718.

See Secs. on the nature and progress of poetry, on rules, and on various kinds of poetry and drama. Part II published in *Critical essays,* ed. Durham, New Haven, 1915.

Gildon, C.: Essay on the art, rise, and progress of the stage in Greece, Rome, and England . . . In Shakespeare's Works, London, 1714, IX.

Also eds. 1725, 1728.

[Gildon, C.?]: Examen miscellaneum. Consisting of verse and prose . . . London . . . 1702.

See especially the *Preface* on poetry.

[Gildon, C.]: The lawe of poetry as laid down by the Duke of Buckinghamshire in his Essay on poetry, by the Earl of Roscommon in his essay on translated verse, and by Lord Landsowne in Unnatural flights in poetry, explain'd and illustrated. London . . . 1721.

[Gildon, C.]: Miscellaneous letters and essays on several subjects . . . London . . . 1694.

Contains *An apology for poetry, Reflections on Rymer's Short view of tragedy, An essay at a vindication of love in tragedies,* against *Rapin and Mr. Rymer* etc.

Godly Sarah . . . Edinburgh . . . 1737.

See especially Preface on genius in poetry.

Godwin, William: The enquirer . . . London . . . 1797.

See especially Part I, essays v and vi on reading and on the classics; Part II on English style.

Goldshmith, Oliver: The art of poetry. See Newbery, John.

[Goldsmith, Oliver]: An enquiry into the present state of polite learning in Europe . . . London . . . 1759.

See especially the chapters *Of criticism* and *Of the stage.* See *Critical review* VII, 369. 2nd. ed. 1774.

Goldsmith, O.: Essays . . . London, 1765.

See especially essay vii on educating the young in literature, oratory, etc. Also eds. 1789, and in *Miscellaneous works,* Perth, 1792.

Goldsmith, O.: Life of Richard Nash, Esq., London, 1762.

See opening paragraphs on biography.

Goldsmith, O.: See Transactions of the Royal Irish Academy; The bee; The public ledger; The British magazine.

Granville, George [Baron Lansdowne]: Essay upon unnatural flights in poetry. Included in The laws of poetry, London, 1721.

Gray's Inn Journal: No. 1, 1754, on burlesque poetry, attributed of Arthur Murphy.

[Greene, Edward Burnaby]: Critical essays . . . London . . . 1770.

See especially the *Observations on the Sublime of Longinus.* See *Critical review* XXX, 233—34.

Green, Edward Burnaby: An essay on pastoral poetry. In Francis Fawkes, The Idylliums of Theocritus, tr. from Greek . . . London . . . 1767.

See *Critical review* XXVI, 17.

Guardian, The: No. xii, March 25, 1713, on criticism, attributed to Steele; No. xv, March 28, 1713, on love verses, easy writing, attributed to Steele; No. xxviii, xxx, xxxii, April 13, 15, 17, 1713, on pastoral poetry, attributed to Steele; No. lxxxvi,

1713, Beauty in poetry, attributed to Steele; No.
clxiv, September 18, 1713, on translations, attributed to Eusden.

H., J.: See Highmore, Joseph.

Hampson, John: See Vida.

Harlequin-Horace, on the art of modern poetry: See
Miller, James.

Harpur, Joseph: An essay on the principles of philosophical criticism applied to poetry . . . London . . .
1810.

Harris, James: Philological inquiries in three parts . . .
London . . . 1781.

> See especially chapters on criticism, on poetics, dramaturgy,
> and diction. Also ed. 1802; Fr. tr. 1789.

[Harris, James]: Upon the rise and progress of criticism
[? London, 1752].

Harte, Walter: An essay on satire particularly on the
Dunciad . . . to which is added, A discourse on
satires, arraigning persons by name, By Monsieur
Boileau. London . . . 1730.

Hawkins, Thomas: The origins of the English drama illustrated in its various species, viz. mystery, morality,
tragedy and comedy . . . Oxford . . . 1773.

> See *Preface*. See *Critical review* XXXV, 349.

Hayley, William: An essay on epic poetry in five epistles to the Reverend Mr. Mason [in verse] . . . London
. . . 1782.

> Also ed. Dublin, 1782.

Hayley, William: Essay on history; in three epistles [in
verse]; to Edward Gibbon Esq. . . . London . . . 1780.

> See especially the lines in Epistle I on the relation between
> history and poetry, and in Epistle III on the laws of history
> and style.

Hayley, William: The triumphs of temper; a poem . . . London . . . 1781.

See *Preface* on comic and satiric poetry.

Hedelin, Francis: The whole art of the stage. Containing not only rules of drammatick art, but many curious observations about it; tr. from French . . . London, 1684.

Also eds. La practique du théâtre, Paris, 1657; Amsterdam, 1715.

Hemsterhuis, M. F.: Œuvres philosophiques . . . Paris . . . 1792.

Henry, Thomas: Twenty essays on the advantages of literature and philosophy in general, and especially on the consistency of literary and philosophical with commercial pursuits . . . Dublin . . . 1791.

See also *Memoirs of the Manchester literary and philosophical society.*

[? Heppesley, John]: A dissertation on comedy in which the rise and progress of that species of drama is particularly consider'd and deduc'd from the earliest to the present age. By a student of Oxford, London . . . 1750.

Heron, Robert, pseud.: See Pinkerton, John.

H[ighmore], J[oseph]: Essays, moral, religious, and miscellaneous . . . London . . . 1766.

Contains essay *On perspicuity in speaking and writing.*

[Hill, Aaron]: The art of acting . . . London . . . 1746.

See especially the dedicatory epistle.

Hill, Aaron: Works . . . London, 1773.

See IV, 355, *An essay on the art of acting.*

Hill, J.: The actor: a treatise on the art of playing, interspersed with theatrical anecdotes, critical re-

marks on plays, and occasional observations on
audiences . . . London . . . 1750.

"By J. Hill M. D. calling himself Sir J. Hill." — *Brit. Mus. Cat.*
See Part I, *Of the principal advantages which a player ought
to have from nature* (sensibility, fire, etc). Part II, *Of those
assistances which players ought to receive from art* (truth of
action, truth of recitation, etc.). See *Monthly review* III, 189.
Also ed. 1755.

Hill, John: See Transactions of the Royal Society of
Edinburgh.

Hill, Robert: Poems on several occasions . . . London . . .
1775.

See especially 284 on the harmony between poetry and painting
and on the decay of tragedy and the growth of the comedy.

Historical memoir of Italian tragedy: See Walker, J. C.

Hoare, Prince: The artist; a collection of essays on
printing, poetry, sculpture, architecture, the drama
. . . London . . . 1810.

See particularly No. v *On dramatic style* by Cumberland.

Hogarth, William: Analysis of beauty, written with a
view of fixing the fluctuating ideas of taste . . .
London . . . 1753.

Also ed. ? 1791.

Holmes, John: The art of rhetoric made easy: or, the
elements of oratory. Being the substance of Dionysius
Longinus' celebrated Treatise on the sublime . . .
London . . . 1739.

See especially the *Preface* and the *Introduction*. Also eds.:
1755, 1766, 1786, 1806, etc.

Home, Henry, Lord Kames: Elements of criticism . . .
Edinburgh . . . 1762.

Preface dated 1761. See also *Animadversions upon Elements of
criticism by H. Home* ... London ... 1771, By Elphinston,
James. See *Critical review* XXXI, 467. 2nd ed., with additions,

88   Literature and Drama.

1763; 4th ed., with additions, 1769; 6th ed., with the author's
last corrections and additions, 1785; 7th ed. 1788. Ger. tr.,
Leipzig, 1763—66 and 1776.

Horace: Ars poetica (Epistola ad Pisones) in Horace's
Works in Latin (printed in England), 1701, 1702,
1711, 1713, 1715, 1717, etc.

See eds. in Latin and English, tr. S. Dunster, 1712, 1729,
1743 etc.; included in Horace's *Works* tr. Creech 1715, 1720,
1737 etc.; tr. W. Popple, 1753; tr. Duncombe 1757—1759; tr.
W. Boscawen 1793—1797. For comment on Hurd ed., 1751,
see E. Gibbon, *Miscellaneous Works*, London, 1796, II, 27.

Hughes, John: An essay on allegorial poetry. Prefixed
to Hughes ed. of Spenser's *Works*, 1715, 1750, etc.

Hughes, John: Poems on several occasions with some
select essays in prose . . . London . . . 1735.

See especially I, 247, *Of style* (dated by Durham, 1698); II,
329, *On descriptions in poetry.*

Hume, David: Essays and treatises on several subjects,
London, 1758.

See especially Part I, 62, Essay xvi, *On Eloquence.*

Hume, David: Four dissertations . . . London . . . 1757.

See especially III, *Of Tragedy.* See *Monthly review* XVI, 122.

Hume, David: Essays, moral and political [and literary]
. . . London . . . 1741.

Also ed. 1742. See also in Hume's *Essays and treatises* . . .
London . . . 1758. Also eds. 1760, 1764, 1768, 1770, 1777,
Dublin 1779, etc. See especially Part I, Essay i *Of delicacy
of taste and passion;* Essay xxv, *Of tragedy* (also included in
Four dissertations, London . . . 1757); Essay xxvi *Of the
standard of taste* (also included in *Four Dissertations*).

[Hurd, Richard]: A discourse concerning poetical imitation. Appended to Hurd's ed. of Horace's Epistola
ad Angustum . . . London . . . 1751.

See also *A discourse etc.* in his *Works* II, 217., London, 1811.

Hurd, Richard: A letter to Mr. Mason on the marks of
imitation . . . Cambridge . . . 1757.

Also in commentary on Horace's *Ars poetica,* 1776. See *Monthly
review* XVIII, 114. See also Hurd, *Reflections on originality
in authors: being remarks on a letter to Mr. Mason on the
marks of imitation: in which the absurd defects of that perfor-
mance are pointed out* . . . London . . . 1766. See *Monthly
review* XXI, 395.

[Hurd, Richard]: Letters on chivalry and romance . . .
London . . . 1762.

Also ed. 1762 Dublin, and several eds. with his *Moral and
political dialogues,* London, 1765, 1771, 1776, 1788.

[Hurd, Richard]: Two dissertations: the one on the pro-
vinces of the several species of dramatic poetry;
the other on poetical imitation. In Q. Horatii Flacci
Epistolæ ad Pisones et Augustum [ed. Hurd] . . .
London . . . 1753.

Also eds. 1766, 1776. See *Monthly review* IX, 11—33.

Hurdis, James: Lecture shewing the several sources of
that pleasure which the human mind receives from
poetry . . . London, 1797.

Idler, The: No. 36, December 23, 1758, The terrifick
diction, by S. Johnson. No. 77, October 6, 1759,
On the familiar style, by S. Johnson.

Inquiry into the propriety of the rules prescribed
for pastoral poetry. Appended to Ramsay, Gentle
Shepherd . . . Edinburgh . . . 1808.

[Isle André, Ives Marie de l']: The art of conversing,
tr. from the French . . . London . . . 1777.

[Israeli, Isaac D']: Curiosity of literature . . . London
. . . 1791—1794.

See especially essays on *Criticism, Taste, Imitators, Belles
Lettres, Metaphors, Innovation, Translation, Literary composition.*
3rd ed. 1793; 4th ed. 1798—1817 with additions; 7th ed. 1827;

etc. *Monthly review* VII N. S., 270; XII N. S., 177 etc., 276 etc.; XVI N. S., 415.

Israeli, Isaac D': A defence of poetry . . . 2nd ed. corrected. Appended to D'Israeli, Specimens of a new version of Telemachus, London . . . 1790.

Israeli, I. D': A dissertation on anecdotes . . . London . . . 1793.

> See *Monthly review* XIII N. S., 279.

Israeli, I[saac] D': An essay on the manners and genius of the literary character . . . London . . . 1795.

> See especially II and XI on literature and modes of literary criticism; IV, V, VII, VIII, IX on genius. See *Monthly review* XVIII N. S., 380.

Israeli, I[saac] D': Miscellanies; or literary recreations . . . London . . . 1796.

> See especially the *Preface, On style, On diaries, Self-biography* etc., *On poetical opuscula, On poetical expression, On literary genius, On novelty in literature*, etc. See *Monthly review* XXIV N. S., 374.

Introduction to the polite arts and sciences, An, including the principles of literature and the belles lettres, London . . . 1763.

Jackson, William: The four ages, together with essays on various subjects . . . London . . . 1798.

> See 311 *On rhyme;* 355 *On the joining of poetry and music;* 441 *On poetical and musical ear.* See *Critical review* XXII N. S., 262; *Monthly review* XXVI N. S., 190.

[Jackson, William]: Thirty letters on various subjects . . . London . . . 1783.

> See especially xiii and xiv on reading and drama. See *Monthly review* LXVIII, 391; *Gentleman's Magazine* LIII, 332. Also eds. 1784 and 1795 with additions and corrections.

Jacob, Hildebrand: Of the sister arts . . . London . . . 1734.

[Jenyns, S.]: The art of dancing, a poem in three cantos . . . London . . . 1729.

Johnson, Samuel: A dissertation upon pastoral poetry. In the Works of Virgil, ed. J. Warton, London, 1753.

See especially I, 35. Also ed. 1765.

Johnson, Samuel: Lives of the poets. In Prefaces, biographical and critical to the works of the English poets . . . London . . . 1779.

See especially the part of *Cowley* on the ode and on metaphysical poetry; *Dryden* on translation; *Milton* on the pastoral and *Akenside* on blank verse. See also numerous scattered dicta on literature and æsthetics, collected by J. E. Brown in *The critical opinions of Samuel Johnson*, Princeton [N. J.], 1926.

Johnson, Samuel: The plays of William Shakespeare . . . to which are added notes by Samuel Johnson, London, 1765.

See *Preface* on rules of drama.

Johnson, Samuel: Rasselas, London . . . 1759.

See especially Chaps. VII and X on the poet's use of nature.

Johnson, S.: See Annual register, Gentleman's magazine, Idler, and Rambler.

Johnson, S.: See Brumoy, P., and Potter, R.

Kames, Lord: See Home, Henry.

[Kausch, John Joseph]: Ästhetische Gespräche über die größesten dichterischen Vorurtheile, Maschinenwerk, Reim und Silbenmaas . . . Breslau u. Leipzig, 1786.

See *Monthly review* LXXIX, 655—57.

Kirby, Thomas: An essay on criticism . . . London, 1758.

Kirkpatrick, J.: The sea-piece . . . London . . . 1750.

See the *Preface* on "nautic" poetry.

[Knox, Vicesimus]: Essays, moral and literary, London . . . 1778.

In 2nd ed. see especially Vol. I, iv. *On eloquence*, vii *On style;* Vol. II, i *On essay writing*, x *On conversation*, xiv *On satire*, xxi *On biography*, xxvi *On prose style*, xxxvii *On speculative*

criticism and on genius. See *Monthly review* LXII, 61; LXVIII,
304. 2nd ed. enlarged 1779; eds. 1782, 1785, 1787, 1791,
N. Y. 1793, etc. 16th ed. 1808.

Knox, Vicesimus: Liberal education ... London ... 1781.
See Sec. xxii *On literature.* See *Monthly review* LXV, 1.
4th ed. 1782, 6th ed. 1784, 9th ed. 1788.

Kollman, Augustus Frederic Christoph: An essay on musical harmony ... London ... 1796.
On music in relation to language.

L., R.: See Lloyd, Robert.

Labe, J. N.: See Maury, Abbé.

Lady's Magazine: XI, 1780, 375, Thoughts on novel writing and reading; XIV, 1783, 372, A few thoughts
on tragedy; XV, 1784, 207, Advantages of modern
tragedy; XV, 1784, 353, Mrs. Brooke: Thoughts on
poetry; XVIII, 1787, 456, General observations on
modern novels; XVIII, 1787, 538, On the epistolary
mode of novel writing; XX, 1789, 290, On the
prevalence of acting in private families; XXI, 1790,
425, 472, On acting private plays. XXII, 1791, 198,
On poetry, by C. S.; XXIII, 1792, 85, On the decline
of poetical taste and genius (from Juvenile excur-
sions in literature and criticism).

Lady's Monthly Museum: I, 1798, 258, 434, On novels;
V, 1800, 215, Hints to novel writers.

Laharpe, J. F.: Lycée, ou cours de littérature ... Paris
... 1799.
See *Monthly review* XXXIII N. S., 449.

Lamotte, Charles: An essay upon poetry and painting
with an appendix concerning obscurity in writing
and painting ... London ... 1730.
Also ed. Dublin 1742.

[Langhorne, John]: The effusions of friendship and fancy
... London ... 1763.
See especially Essay XXXIV on drama. Also ed. 1766.

Langhorne, John: Letters of friendship . . . London . . . 1770.

See especially letters 13, 15, and 37, on poetry.

[Langhorne, John]: Letters on the eloquence of the pulpit . . . London . . . 1765.

See especially Letter II on *Style of composition,* and III on *Elocution.*

Lansdowne: See Gildon, C., and Granville, George.

Laws of poetry as laid down by the Duke of Buckinghamshire, The: See Gildon, C.

Le Clerc [Jean?]: Parrhasiana: or thoughts upon several subjects, as criticism, history, morality and politics; tr. London . . . 1700.

Lévesque, P. C.: See Mémoires de l'Institut national.

Letter to His Excellency Count [?Caylus] on poetry, painting and sculpture, A. . . . London . . . 1768.

See *Critical review* XXVI, 387.

Letters by writers of distinguished merit: See Newbery, John.

Letters concerning poetical translations and Virgil's and Milton's arts of verse: See Benson, William.

Letters on chivalry and romance: See Hurd, R.

Letters on the drama: See Penn, John.

Letters on the eloquence of the pulpit: See Langhorne, J.

Lévesque, P. C.: See Mémoires de l'Institut national.

L[loyd], R[obert]: The actor, a poetical epistle to Bonnell Thornton . . . London . . . 1760.

Lloyd, Robert: Poetical works . . . London . . . 1774.

See II, 1. *A dialogue between the author and his friend;* 17, *The poet;* 105, *On rhyme.*

Lloyd, Robert: The poetry professors. In Works of Lloyd, Anderson's British poets, London, 1795.

See X, 624. Also in Chalmers' *Poets,* London, 1810, etc.

Longinus: A treatise on the sublime . . . with critical
reflections, remarks, and observations, by M. Boileau,
M. Dacier, and M. Boivin . . . London . . . 1712
[tr. into English].

See *The works of Longinus, or a treatise concerning the sover-
eign perfection of writing;* tr. from the Greek with some remarks on the English poets, by Mr. Welsted . . . London . . .
1712. Also ed. 1724. See also *Dionysius Longinus: On the
sublime, tr. from the Greek with notes . . . and some account
of the life, writings and character of the author,* by W. Smith,
London, 1739. See also Greene, E. B.

Lounger, The: (edited by Mac Kenzie) I, No. 20, 1785,
168, On novel writing; No. 27, 1785, 230, An
examination of the moral effects of tragedy (continued in No. 28, 237). II, No. 49, 1785, 121,
Observations on comedy (continued in No. 50, 131,
Moral effects).

Lyrical ballads: See Wordsworth, William.

Macaroni and theatrical magazine, 1773, 361, Painting
and poetry compared.

Mac Laurin, John (of Dreghorn): Works . . . Edinburgh
. . . 1798.

See remarks on poetry in Vol. II. See also *Critical review* XXV,
(1798), 435.

[Madan, Judith] (née Cooper): The progress of poetry.
In the Flowerpiece: a collection of miscellany poems
. . . London . . . 1731.

See p. 130—141. Also in *The poetical calendar,* 1763, and
apparently published separately in 1782 or 1783. See also
Gentleman's magazine LIII, 152.

Mainwaring, John: See Mathias, T. J.

Mainwaring, John: Sermons on several occasions; to
which is prefixed, a dissertation on that species
of composition, Cambridge, 1780.

Manchester Literary and Philosophical Society: See Memoirs.

[Mangin, Edward?]: Essay on the sources of the pleasures received from literary compositions, London
. . . 1809.

Includes essays on taste, the imagination, the sublime, terror, pity, melancholy, beauty, the ludicrous etc. 2nd ed. London, 1813.

Manwaring, Edward: Historical and critical account of the most eminent classic authors, London . . . 1737.

Manwaring, Edward: Of harmony and numbers, in Latin and English prose, and in English poetry . . . London
. . . 1744.

Manwaring, Edward: Stychology; or a recovery of the Latin, Greek and Hebrew numbers . . . London . . . 1737.

Marmontel, J. F.: Elements de littérature . . . Paris . . . 1787.

Martinus scriblerus: See Swift, J.

Martyn, John: Pub. Virgilii Maronis Georgicorum libri quatuor . . . London . . . 1741.

See especially the *Preface* for comments on didactic poetry. Also eds. 1746, 1755, 1811, etc. See also *Pub. Virgilii Maronis bucolicorum ecolgæ decem* . . . London . . . 1749 (particularly the *Preface* on pastoral poetry). Also ed. 1813.

[Mason, John]: An essay on elocution or pronunciation. Intended chiefly for the assistance of those who instruct others in the art of reading and those who are often called to speak in publick, London . . . 1748.

2nd ed. 1748, 3rd 1751, 4th 1761.

[Mason, John]: An essay on the power of numbers and the principles of harmony in poetical compositions, London . . . 1749.

Also ed. 1761. See *Monthly review* II, 68.

[Mason, John]: An essay on the power and harmony of prosaic numbers, London . . . 1761.

[Mathias, Thomas James]: The pursuits of literature: a satirical poem . . . London . . . 1794—97.

See especially the *Introductory letter.* 6th ed. 1798. See Main-waring, John: *Remarks on The pursuits of literature* [by T. J. Mathias] . . . *London* . . . *1798;* Burdon, William: *An exami-nation of the merits and tendency of the pursuits of literature* . . . *Cambridge* . . . *1799.* Also *Monthly review* XXXI N. S., 443, and XXXII, 441. See also *Monthly review* XXXI N. S., 111: *Impartial strictures on the poem called "Pursuits of Literature."*

Maury, Abbé: The principles of eloquence . . . tr. from French; with additional notes, by John Neal Labe . . . London . . . 1793.

Originally *Discours choisis*, Paris, 1777. See *Monthly review* XII N. S., 147; LVII, 309.

Melmoth, Courtney: Observations on the Night thoughts of Dr. Young; with occasional remarks on the beauties of poetical composition . . . London . . . 1776.

Mémoires de l'Institut national . . . Paris . . . 1798.

See Pierre Charles Lévesque on ancient tragic poets. See *Monthly review* XXXI N. S., 460.

Memoirs of the Manchester literary and philosophical society: I, 1785, 7: Henry, Thos., F. R. S., On the advantages of literature and philosophy in general, and especially on the consistency of literary and philosophical with commercial pursuits (read 1781); I, 54: Barnes, Thomas, D. D., On the nature and essential characters of poetry as distinguished from prose (read 1781). For later edition see Barnes, T., Dublin, 1791; III, 1790, 307: Sharp, Richard, On the nature and utility of eloquence; IV, 1793, 96, Aiken, J., On the impression of reality attending dramatic representations. See Monthly review XII N. S., 18; V, Part II, 1798, p. 319. Walker, Rev. George, F. R. S., On tragedy and the interest in tragical representations: an essay.

Mercer, Thomas: Poems . . . Edinburgh . . . 1774.

See 103 *Of Poetry: an epistolary essay.*

[Mercier, Louis Sebastien]: De la littérature et des littérateurs suivi d'un nouvel examen de la tragédie françoise . . . Yverdon, 1778.

[Mercier, Louis Sebastien]: Du théâtre ou nouvel essai sur l'art dramatique . . . Amsterdam . . . 1773.

Michaelis: See Annual register.

Microcosm, The: 1787, No. xxii, 254, On poetry as an art; No. xxvi, 294, On novel writing.

Miller, George: See Transactions of the Royal Irish Academy.

[Miller, James]: Harlequin-Horace, or the art of modern poetry . . . London . . . 1731.

Also 1735, 1773 in Ruddiman's *Collection of curious pieces.*

Miscellaneous letters and essays on several subjects: See Gildon, C.

[Mitford, W.]: An essay upon the harmnoy of language, intended principally to illustrate that of the English language . . . London . . . 1774.

Chiefly a study of English metrics. See especially Sec. xiii, *Of the connexion of poetry with music.* See *Critical review* XXXVIII, 137. 2nd ed. with large additions 1804.

Monboddo, Lord: See Burnet, James.

Monthly review: X, 385 On epic poetry; XV, 128, On literature and morals; LVII, 89, On literary criticism; LXVII, 262, On copyist poets; XII N. S., 361, On prose style in latter 18th century.

See also under authors reviewed.

[Moor, James]: Essays read to a literary society within the college at Glasgow . . . Glasgow . . . 1759.

See especially *On historical composition.* See *Critical review* IX, 177.

Moor, James: On the end of tragedy, according to Aristotle; an essay, in two parts . . . Glasgow . . . 1763.

Also ed. 1794.

Moor, James: See also Aristotle.

Morrice: The amour of Venus . . . London . . . 1732.

See especially the *Preface* on painting and poetry.

[Morris, C.]: An essay toward fixing true standards of wit, humour, raillery, satire and ridicule . . . London . . . 1744.

There is appended an essay, *Concerning humour in comedy.*

Morvan de Bellegarde, Jean Baptiste: Reflexions upon Ridicule . . . London . . . 1706.

French eds. 1696, 1699 etc. Also Eng. eds. 1707, 1717, 1727, 1739. See Fielding's *Joseph Andrews, Preface.*

Motte, Houdart de la: Odes, avec un discours sur la poésie en général et sur l'ode en particulier . . . Paris . . . 1709.

Motte, Houdart de la: Œuvres de théâtre; avec plusiers discours sur la tragédie . . . Paris . . . 1730.

Motte, Houdart de la: Réflexions sur la critique . . . Paris . . . 1715.

Motte, Houdart de la: Suites réflexions sur la tragédie, où l'on répond à M. de Voltaire . . . Paris . . . 1730.

Mulgrave, Earl of: See Sheffield.

Murphy, A.: See Gray's Inn Journal.

Neuville, Chicaneau de: Considérations sur les ouvrages d'esprit . . . Paris . . . 1758.

New annual register: See Warton, J.

[Newbery, John]: The art of poetry made easy . . . being the seventh volume of The circle of the sciences etc. . . . London . . . 1746.

[Newbery, John]: The art of poetry on a new plan, illustrated with a great variety of examples. [Sometimes attributed to Oliver Goldsmith] 2 vols. London, 1762.

See especially the *Introduction* on origin, thoughts and styles of poetry followed by detailed discussion of types, epigram, epitaph, elegy, epistle, descriptive poetry etc. See Chap. XX *Of dramatic poetry.* See *Critical review* XIII, 429.

[Newbery, John]: The art of rhetorick laid down in an easy manner, being the sixth volume of The circle of the sciences, &c. . . . London . . . 1745.

Also eds. 1769, 1776.

[Newbery, John?]: Letters by writers of distinguished merit; with many original letters and cards by the editor, who has also prefixed a dissertation on epistolary style . . . the fourth edition . . . London . . . 1758.

Also 5th ed. 1760; also ed. 1787.

[Newburgh, B.]: Essays, political, moral and critical . . . Dublin . . . 1769.

See introductory letter to the Provost and Fellows of the university of Dublin.

[Nichols, J.]: Select collection of poems with notes . . . London . . . 1780.

See especially III, 217 *et seq.* note on allegory.

Normandy, Marquis of: See Sheffield, John.

Nougaret: De l'art du théâtre . . . Paris . . . 1769.

Nourse, Mr.: Ut Pictura Poesis [1741]. In Dodsley's Collection . . . London . . . 1758, V, 93—95.

Observations on poetry: See Pemberton, Henry.

Ode on beauty, An: See Cooke, William.

Ode on benevolence with observations on education, taste and poetry, An . . . London . . . 1753.

Ode on poetry, printing and sculpture, An: See Cooke, Wm.

Ode on the powers of eloquence: See Cooke, Wm.
Ode on the powers of poetry, An: See Cooke, Wm.
[Ogden, James]: The revolution . . . London . . . 1790.

See especially *Introductory essay on poetry and particularly upon the epic.*

Ogilvie, John: A critical dissertation on epic machinery. In Britannia . . . Aberdeen . . . 1801.

Ogilvie, John: An essay on the lyric poetry of the ancients. In Poems . . . London . . . 1762.

See *Critical review* XIV, 293. Also eds. 1764 and 1769.

Ogilvie, John: Poems . . . London . . . 1769.

See especially the *Preface* on literary criticism, and the *Introduction* to *Providence* on allegory.

Ogilvie, John: Rona, a Poem . . . London . . . 1777.

See especially the *Introduction* on poetry.

Ogilvie, John: Philosophical and critical observations on the nature, characters and various species of composition . . . London, 1774.

See *Critical review* XXXVIII, 81.

Oldmixon, J.: Essay on criticism; as it regards design, thought, and expression. In prose and verse . . . London . . . 1728.

On poetry: a rapsody: See Swift, J.

[Parnell, Thomas]: An essay on the different stiles of poetry . . . London . . . 1713.

Parnell, Thomas, Archdeacon of Clogher: An essay on the life, writings and learning of Homer. In Pope's tr. of the Iliad, London, 1715.

Especially on narrative style in poetry. Also eds. 1720, 1729, 1736, 1750, 1760, 1763, etc.

Parnell, Dr. Thomas: Posthumous works . . . London . . . 1758.

See especially *The gift of poetry*, on literary genius.

Parrhasiana: See Le Clerc.

[Passeri, G. B.]: Della istituzione de' poeti. In Nuova raccolta d'opuscoli, Venezia, 1768.

[Pemberton, Henry]: Observation on poetry, especially the epic . . . London . . . 1738.

Penn, John: Critical poetical and dramatic works . . . London . . . 1798.

> See especially *Art of English poetry,* preface and notes. See *Critical review* XXIV N. S., 475.

[Penn, John]: Letters on the drama, London . . . 1796.

> See especially letters on taste, poetical probability, imitation, chorus, unities, tragi-comedy, etc.

Percival, Thomas: Moral and literary dissertations . . . London, 1784.

> See especially, *On inconsistency of expectation in literary pursuits; On taste for the fine arts;* and *On the alliance of natural history and philosophy with poetry.* See *Monthly review* LXXII, 177. 2nd ed. "revised and enlarged," 1789.

[Pinkerton, John] Heron, Robert [pseud.]: Letters of literature . . . London . . . 1785.

> See especially the letters on barbaric poetry. See *Monthly review* LXXIV, 175.

Plain dealer, The: Vol. II, 1734. No. 60, p. 20, Poets and painters compared; No. 70, p. 107, Of stile and oratory.

The players: A satire . . . London . . . 1733.

Poetry made familiar and easy to young gentlemen and ladies . . . London . . . 1769.

> See especially Chapter I on the definition of poetry and the qualifications of a true poet.

[Polwhele, Richard]: The art of eloquence: a didactic poem. Book the first . . . London . . . 1785.

> See especially the prose *Advertisement.* See *Monthly review* LXXIII, 231.

Polwhele, Richard: The English orator . . . the second
edition . . . Exeter . . . 1786.

Books II and III published 1787.

[Pope, Alexander]: Essay on criticism . . . London . . .
1711.

Second ed. 1713. Other eds. 1717, 1722, 1751 etc. Latin tr.
1782. See Dennis, John, *Reflections critical and satyrical, upon
a late rhapsody call'd an Essay upon criticism* . . . *London* . . .
[1711].

Pope [Alexander]: An epistle to the Right Honourable
Richard Earl of Burlington. Occasion'd by his
publishing Palladio's designs . . . London . . . 1731.

Also 3rd ed. 1731; Dublin 1732. Appears in Pope's works as
Epistle IV, *Of false taste*. See also Bramston's *Man of taste
occasion'd by an epistle of Mr. Pope's on that subject*, London
. . . 1733.

Pope [Alexander]: The Iliad of Homer . . . London . . .
1715.

See *Preface* on epic poetry.

Pope, Alexander: Odyssey . . . London . . . 1726.

See *Postscript* on epic and mock-epic poetry.

Pope, A.: See Theobald, L.
Popple, W.: See Horace.
Porte, Joseph de la: Ecole de littérature . . . Paris . . .
1764.

Vol. I, on rhetoric and poetics with special attention to various
kinds such as criticism, oratory, translation etc., and Vol. II,
on types of poetry and drama.

Porte [Joseph] de la: Extrait de l'essai sur la peinture,
la sculpture, et l'architecture tiré de ses observations sur la littérature moderne . . . [? Paris], 1751.

Porter, John: A critical essay upon epistolary and elegiac
poetry. In The Platonic lovers [3d ed.] . . . London
. . . 1732.

[Potter, Robert]: The art of criticism as exemplified in Dr. Johnson's lives of the most eminent English poets . . . London . . . 1789.

See especially the appended *Dream,* a dialogue between Dr. Johnson and Dr. Warton on literary criticism.

Potter, Robert: An inquiry into some passages in Dr. Johnson's Lives of the poets: particularly his observations on lyric poetry . . . London . . . 1783.

Powers of the pen, The. A poem addressed to John Curre, Esqr. . . . London . . . 1766.

Present state of the literati: a satire [in verse] London . . . 1752.

On poetry, history-writing, etc. See *Monthly review* VI, 316.

Preston, William: See Transactions of the Royal Irish Academy.

Priestley, Joseph: A course of lectures on the theory of language and universal grammar . . . Warrington . . . 1762.

See especially lecture XV, on translation; XVI, on metrical composition, and XVII on precision, harmony etc. of words.

Priestley, Joseph: A course of lectures on oratory and criticism, London, 1777.

Written in 1762. See especially Part III on taste, the passions, the pleasures of the imagination, and the sublime. See *Monthly review* LVII, 89. Also an ed. in Priestley's *Theological and miscellaneous works* [London . . . 1817—1831], Vol. XXIII, 253.

Priestley, Joseph: The rudiments of English grammar; . . . with observations on style . . . London . . . 1761.

Also eds. 1768, 1772, 1789 (revised), 1798, etc.

Principles of literature: See Introduction to the polite arts and sciences, An.

Progress of poetry, The: See Madan, Judith.

Progress of satire, The: An essay in verse: See Bos-
cawen, W.
Public ledger, The: London, 1760: Chinese letters No. 40,
on English versification, ascribed O. Goldsmith.
Nos. 63 and 97, on literature, O. Goldsmith. Col-
lected as The citizen of the world, London, 1762.
Pursuits of literature, The: See Mathias, T. J.
Quincy, John: Holdsworth's Muscipula translated . . .
London . . . 1714.

See especially *Preface* on burlesque.

Rambler: I, March 20, 1750, on periodical literature,
ascribed to Dr. Johnson. III, March 27, 1750, on
literature and literary criticism, Dr. Johnson. IV,
March 31, 1750, on romances, Dr. Johnson. XXII,
June 2, 1750, on wit and learning, Dr. Johnson.
XXIII, June 5, 1750, contrariety of criticism,
Dr. Johnson. XXXVI, July 21, 1750, reasons why
pastorals delight, Dr. Johnson. XXXVII, July 24,
1749, true principles of pastoral poetry, Dr. Johnson
(reprinted in J. Warton's ed. of Virgil, 1753 etc.
See Courtney and Smith, Bibliography of Johnson,
Oxford, 1925, p. 25). LX, October 13, 1750, on
biography, Dr. Johnson. LXXXVIII and XC, on English metrics. XCIII, February 5, 1751, on literary
criticism, Dr. Johnson. XCIV, March 16, 1751, on
literary criticism, Dr. Johnson. CXXI, May 4, 1751,
Dangers of imitation, Dr. Johnson. CXXV, May 28,
1751, Difficulty of defining comedy. CLII, August 31,
1751, on letter-writing. CLVI, September 7, 1751,
Laws of writing not always indisputable; reflections
on tragi-comedy, Dr. Johnson. CLVIII, September 21,
1751, on lyric poetry. CLXVIII, October 26, 1751,
poetry debased by mean expressions. CLXXVI, November 23, 1751, on literary criticism, Dr. Johnson.
Ramsay, A.: See Inquiry into pastoral poetry.

Rapin [René]: Discourse of pastorals. In Idylliums of Theocritus . . . Oxford . . . 1684.

Also ed. 1721.

Rapin, René: Reflections on Aristotle's treatise of poesie containing the necessary, rational and universal rules for epick, dramatick, and the other sorts of poetry [tr. T. Rymer] . . . London . . . 1674.

Also ed. 1794. Original Fr. ed. 1674.

Rapin [René]: The whole critical works of Monsieur Rapin . . . newly translated into English by several hands . . . London . . . 1706.

See especially the *Reflections on eloquence* and *On Aristotle's treatise of poesie.* Also tr. 1672 and tr. B. Kennet, 1716.

Rapin, René: Reflexions sur la poétique d'Aristote [Paris?], 1674.

Reason, a poem, to which is prefixed a notion of poetry: an essay . . . London . . . 1759.

See *Monthly review* XVIII, 651. See also *Critical review* VI, 171.

Reeve, Clara: The progress of romance . . . Colchester . . . 1785.

Reflections upon the eloquence of these times: See Rapin, René.

Reid, Thomas: Essays on the intellectual powers of man . . . Edinburgh . . . 1785.

See essay viii, *Of taste.*

Remarks on some observations on Dr. Brown's dissertation on poetry and music: See Dr. Brown.

Richards, George: An essay on the characteristic differences between ancient and modern poetry, and the several causes from which they result [Oxford, 1789].

See especially the early paragraphs on genius.

[Richardson, William]: Cursory remarks on tragedy . . .
London . . . 1714.

Sometimes attributed to Edward Taylor. See especially the
Introduction.

Richardson, William: See Transactions of the Royal
Society of Edinburgh.

[Robertson, Joseph]: An essay on the nature of English
verse, with directions for reading poetry . . . London
. . . 1799.

Rolli, P. A.: See Voltaire.

Rollin, Charles: The method of teaching and studying
the belles lettres, or an introduction to languages,
poetry, rhetoric . . . with reflections on taste . . .
third edition, London . . . 1742.

The original French ed., *De la manière etc.*, came out in Paris,
1726—28.

Roscomnon, Earl of: See Gildon, C.

Rousseau, J. J.: Eloisa: or a series of original letters . . .
Dublin . . . 1761.

See especially Letter LXXXII. First French ed. 1761, as *Lettres de deux amants*.

Royal Irish Academy: See Transactions.

Royal Society of Edinburgh: See Transactions.

Saint-Mard, Rémond de: Réflexions sur la poésie . . .
suivies de trois lettres sur la décadence du goût
en France . . . Paris . . . 1733.

Sanderman, Robert: An essay on preaching . . . Edinburgh, 1763.

[Schomberg, Alexander Crowcher], Scriblerus Secundus
[pseud.]: Prolegomena on the poetry of the present
age. In Schomberg's Bagley, a poem, Oxford, 1777.

Scott, John Robert: Dissertations, essays and parallels . . .
London . . . 1800.

See especially *Essay on writing history*.

Scriblerus Secundus [pseud.]: See Schomberg, A. C.

Serle, Ambrose: The art of writing, containing I. Rules
for writing all the hands now in use . . . II. An
explanation of the different hands . . . a new edition
. . . London, 1776.

A sort of advanced school book with æsthetic dicta in the
Preface.

Sharp, Richard: See Memoirs of the Manchester literary
and philosophical Society.

Shenstone, William: Works in verse and prose, London,
1764—1769.

See especially: I, 3, *Essay on elegy;* II, essays *On books, On
writing and books, On books and writers,* in his *Essays on
men, manners and things.*

Sheffield, John, Earl of Mulgrave: An essay on poetry. . .
[2nd ed.] London, 1691.

Also eds. 1697, 1713, 1717, 1794, with *Death,* 1701, 1716, and
in *Works* 1721, 1723 etc. Tr. French 1764.

Sheridan, Thomas: A course of lectures on elocution:
together with two dissertations on language; and
some other tracts relative to those subjects . . .
London . . . 1762.

Sheridan, Thomas: Lectures on the art of reading . . .
London . . . 1775.

See *Monthly review* LII, 399; LIII, 204. See also *Critical
review* XXXIX, 231, 290; XL, 37. Third ed. 1787; sixth
ed. 1805.

[Smalridge, George]: The art of preaching, in imitation
of Horace's Art of poetry . . . London, 1739.

Some observations on Dr. Brown's dissertation on poetry
and music: See Brown, John.

Some rules for speaking and action to be observed at
the bar, in the pulpit . . . the second edition, London
. . . 1716.

Specimen of a commentary on Shakespeare, A: See
Whiter, W.

Spectator: No. 35, April 10, 1711, False wit and humour,
attributed to Addison. No. 39, April 14, 1711, English tragedy, attributed to Addison. No. 40, April 16,
1711, Tragedy and tragi-comedy, attributed to Addison. No. 42, April 18, 1711, English tragedy, attributed to Addison. No. 44, April 20, 1711, Stage
tricks to excite pity, attributed to Addison. No. 51,
April 28, 1711, On the relation of the witty to the
indelicate in comedy, attributed to Steele. No. 58,
May 7, 1711, No. 59, May 8, 1711, No. 60, May 9,
1711, No. 61, May 10, 1711, No. 62, May 11, 1711:
On true and false wit, attributed to Addison. No. 63,
May 12, 1711, Allegory on false and true wit, attributed to Addison. No. 165, On burlesque. No.
208, October 29, 1711, Depraved taste in the theatre, attributed to Steele. No. 407, June 17, 1712,
Gestures in oratory, attributed to Addison. No. 541,
November 20, 1712, On pronunciation and action
(not ascribed). No. 548, November 28, 1712, On
poetical justice (not ascribed). No. 592, September 10, 1714, Dramatic improvements, attributed
to Addison. No. 595, September 17, 1714, On the
abuse of metaphors (not ascribed). No. 616, November 5, 1714, No. 617, November 8, 1714: On
vulgar phrases; on strained and pompous phrases
(not ascribed). No. 618, November 10, 1714, On
epistolary poetry (not ascribed). No. 633, December 15, 1714, On oratory (not ascribed).

Spence [Joseph]: Polymetis: or an enquiry concerning
the agreement between the works of the Roman
poets and the remains of the antient artists . . .
London . . . 1747.

See Dialogue xx on translation. 2nd ed. 1755; 6th ed. 1777,
and several abridged eds. German tr. Wien, 1773—76.

Stack, Richard: See Transactions of the Royal Irish Academy.

[?Steele, Richard]: English grammar with the arts of logic, rhetoric and poetry . . . London . : . 1728.

Steele: See The guardian, The spectator, and The tatler.

Sterne, Lawrence: The life and opinions of Tristram Shandy, Gentleman . . . London . . . 1760—67.

See especially Book III, chap. xii, on the three dramatic unities.

Stevenson, William: See Fénelon, F. de S.

[Stillingfleet, Benjamin; or Fielding, Henry]: Essay on conversation . . . London . . . 1737.

Stockdale, Percival: Inquiry into the nature and genuine laws of poetry; including a particular defence of the writings and genius of Mr. Pope ... London ... 1778.

A reply to Warton's *Essay on the writings and genius of Pope.* See *Monthly review* LIX, 70.

Student of Oxford, A.: Comedy, Dissertation on, in which which the rise and progress of that species of the drama in particularly considered and deduced from the earliest to the present age. By a student of Oxford, London, 1750.

[?Swift, J.]: On poetry: a rapsody, London, 1733.

Ed. Dublin, 1734. (Title page says that the 1st ed. was in Dublin also.)

[Swift, J. (with Pope and Arbuthnot)]: Martinus Scriblerus, ΠΕΡΙ ΒΑΘΟΥΕ: or the art of sinking in poetry . . . London . . . 1727.

Pope, A., *Works,* ed. Warburton, 1751. VI, 195.

Taste, an epistle to a young critic: See Armstrong, John.

Tatler: No. 165, April 29, 1710, Impertinence of criticism, attributed to Addison. No. 8, April 28, 1709, Reformation of the stage, attributed to Steele. No. 32, June 23, 1709, On punning, attributed to

Steele. No. 61, August 30, 1709, No. 71, September 22, 1709, On satire, attributed to Steele. No. 63, September 3, 1709, On ridicule, attributed to Steele. No. 98, November 24, 1709, Impressive tendency in poetry, attributed to Steele. No. 106, December 13, 1709, Catalogue of poetical stock, attributed to Steele. No. 115, January 3, 1710, Taste for puppet-shows, attributed to Steele. No. 143, March 9, 1710, Provision for pastorals, attributed to Steele. No. 182, June 8, 1710, On the theatre, attributed to Steele. No. 244, October 31, 1710, On eloquence, attributed to Steele.

Taylor, Edward: See Richardson, William.

Temple, Launcelot: See Armstrong, John.

Temple, Sir William: Miscellanea, the second part . . . London . . . 1690.

> See especially *Of poetry*. 3rd. ed. "corrected and augmented by the author," 1692. See also Temple's *Works*, London, 1720, I, 233.

Thirty letters on various subjects: See Jackson, William.

Thomson, Alexander: The paradise of taste . . . London . . . 1796.

Thomson, Alexander: Pictures of poetry . . . London . . . 1799.

> See *Critical review* XXVII N. S., 260, and *Monthly review* XXXIII N. S., 149.

Tickell, Richard: The wreath of fashion or the art of sentimental poetry . . . London . . . 1778.

Transactions of the Royal Irish Academy, Dublin: I, 1787, Polite Literature, p. 3, An essay on sublimity of writing, by Richard Stack; p. 57, Thoughts on lyric poetry, by William Preston. See Monthly review LXXXI, 48. II, 1788, Polite literature, p. 69, Essay on ridicule, wit and humour, by William Preston. See Monthly review VII N. S., 64—65. V, Polite literature, p. 17, Essay on the origin and nature of our idea of the sublime, by George Miller; p. 39, Essay on ... style in writing considered with respect to thoughts and sentiments as well as words, and indicating the writer's peculiar and characteristic disposition, habits and powers of mind, by Robert Burrowes. VI, 1797, Polite literature; p. 41, Essay on the variations of English prose, from the revolution to the present time, by Thomas Wallace.

See *Critical review* XXVIII, 420. See *Monthly review* XXIX N. S., 15; p. 23, on choice of subjects for tragedy, by W. Preston; p. 24, on English prose, by T. Wallace. See *Annual register*, 1799, 438.

Transactions of the Royal Society of Edinburgh ... Edinburgh ... 1788, Part II, Papers of a literary class, 76 and 181, An essay upon the principles of historical composition, with an application of those principles to the writings of Tacitus, by John Hill. 99, On the dramatic or ancient form of historical composition [read June 21, 1784], by William Richardson.

Trapp, Joseph: Prælectiones poeticæ ... Oxonii ... 1711.

2nd. ed., London, 1722; 3rd., London, 1736; tr. English, *Lectures on Poetry*, London, 1742.

Tremblay, Frain du: Discours sur l'origine de la poésie, sur son usage et sur le bon goût ... Paris ... 1713.

Troublet [N. C. J.]: Essais sur divers sujets de littérature et de morale ... Paris ... 1735.

On discultory writing, conversation, raillery etc. Eds. in French, 1737, 1741, 1749, 1754, etc. In English, 1737, 1743. Also translations into Dutch, German and Italian.

Twining, Thomas: Aristotle's Treatise on poetry, translated with ... two dissertations, on poetical and musical, imitation ... London ... 1789.

See *Monthly review* IV N. S., 383; VII N. S., 121; XI N. S., 241.

Two dissertations on poetry: See Hurd, R.

[Tytler, A. F., Lord Woodhouselee]: Essay on the principles of translation . . . the second edition, corrected . . . London . . . 1797.

Upon the rise and progress of criticism: See Harris, J.

Vida, Marcus Hieronymus, The poetics of, [translated]
By John Hampson . . . London . . . 1793.

See *Monthly review* XIII N. S., 188.

Voltaire: An essay upon the civil wars of France . . .
and also upon the epick poetry of the European
nations from Homer down to Milton . . . London . . .
1727.

2nd. ed., 1728; 4th 1731, etc. It appeared in French, Paris,
1728. See also G. Baretti, *Dissertation upon the Italian poetry*,
1753, and P. A. Rolli, *Remarks upon M. Voltaire's Essay on
the epick poetry of the European nations*, 1728.

Voltaire: Critical essays upon dramatic poetry and the
belles lettres: with remarks on the theatres of the
Italians, Spaniards, English, French, and other nations of Europe . . . Glasgow . . . 1761.

Walker, George: Essays on various subjects . . . London
. . . 1809.

See especially Essay ii, *On tragedy:* x and xi on the machinery
of the ancient epic poem.

Walker, George: See Memoirs of the Manchester literary
and philosophical society.

Walker, John: Elements of elocution. Being the substance of a course of lectures on the art of reading;
delivered at several colleges in the university of
Oxford . . . London . . . 1781.

See *Monthly review* XXXI N. S., 110. Also eds. 1799, and 1810.

Walker, J.: A rhetorical grammar . . . London . . . 1785.

[Walker, Joseph Cooper]: Historical memoir on Italian

tragedy . . . interspersed with occasional observations on the Italian theatres . . . London . . . 1799.

See *Monthly review* XXIX N. S., 1.

Wallace, Thomas: See Transactions of the Royal Irish
Academy.

Walsh, William: Collection of letters and poems . . .
London, 1692.

See especially the *Preface* on love poetry.

Walwyn, B.: An essay on comedy . . . London . . . 1782.

See *Monthly review* LXVI, 308—09.

[Warburton, William]: Discourse on pastoral poetry. In
Pope, Alexander, Works, London, 1751, I, 3.

See also Warburton's notes, especially to the *Essay on Criticism.*

Ward, John: A system of oratory, delivered in a course
of lectures publicly read at Gresham college, London
. . . 1759.

See especially Lectures ii and iii on the nature and divisions
of oratory.

Warton, Joseph: A dissertation on the nature and conduct of the Æneid. In the Works of Virgil . . .
London, 1753.

See especially II, iii, containing æsthetic dicta on epic poetry.
Also ed. 1763.

Warton, Joseph: Essay on the genius and writings of
Pope. 2 vols. . . . London, 1756.

See *Monthly review* XIV. See *Annual register* II N. S., 1782,
94. Also eds. 1762, "corrected" 1772, 1782.

Warton, Joseph: Reflections on didactic poetry. In the
Works of Virgil, London, 1753.

See especially I, 393. Also ed. 1765.

Warton, Thomas: The history of English poetry . . . to
which are prefixed two dissertations. I, On the
origin of romantic fiction in Europe. II, On the

Draper, Eighteenth Century English Æsthetica.

introduction of learning into England . . . London
. . . 1774—1781. [3 vols.]

See *Monthly review* XXXVII, 275; L, 417.

Warton, Thomas: Observations on the Faerie Queene of
Spenser . . . London . . . 1754.

Also eds. 1762 etc.

Watkinson, Edward: See Critical review.
Webb [Daniel]: Literary amusements . . . London . . .
1787.

See especially *Further thoughts on manners and languages* and
Essay on party-writing.

Webb [Daniel]: Observations on the correspondence
between poetry and music . . . London . . . 1769.

See *Critical review* XXVIII, 107.

Webb, Daniel: Remarks on the beauties of poetry . . .
London . . . 1762.

See *Critical review* XIII, 401. Also ed. Dublin, 1764.

Webster [of Christ Church, Oxon.]: The stage: a poem
subscribed to Joseph Addison, Esq. ... London ...
1713.

Weekes, N.: The abuse of poetry. A satire . . . second
edition . . . London . . . 1754.

See especially the *Preface* on critics and criticism.

Welstead, Leonard: Epistles, odes etc. . . . to which is
prefix'd, a dissertation concerning the perfection of
the English language, the state of poetry, etc. . . .
London . . . 1724.

Also in his *Works,* London, 1787. See also Longinus.

Weston, Joseph: An essay on the superiority of Dryden's
versification over that of Pope and the moderns, in
John Morfitt's Philotoxi Ardenæ . . . Birmingham ...
[1789].

See *Monthly review* LXXX, 329.

Whitehead, William: An essay on ridicule . . . London
. . . 1743.

[Whiter, Walter]: A specimen of a commentary on
Shakespeare; containing, 1st Notes on As you like
it; 2dly an attempt to explain and illustrate various
passages in a new principle of criticism, derived
from Mr. Locke's Doctrine of the association of
ideas [? 1798].

See *Monthly review* XXV N. S., 400.

Wilkes [Derrick, Samuel]: General view of the stage . . .
London, 1759.

[Wilkie, William]: The Epigoniad, a poem in rime . . .
Edinburgh . . . 1759.

See especially the *Preface* on epic poetry.

[Withers, Dr.]: Aristarchus, or the principles of composition . . . London . . . [1791].

[Wordsworth, William]: Lyrical Ballads, with a few
other poems, Bristol . . . 1798.

See especially the prefatory *Advertisement.*

[Young, Edward]: Conjectures on original composition
in a letter to the author of Sir Charles Grandison,
London . . . 1759.

Young, Edward: On lyric poetry. In Ocean, an ode . . .
London . . . 1728.

Young, Sir William: [Proposals for] Contemplatio philo-
sophica: a posthumous work of the late Brook Taylor
. . . London . . . 1793.

See the remarks on biography in the *Introduction* to Taylor's life.

Zanotti, Francisco Maria: Dell'arte poetica. In Opere,
Bologna, 1779—1802.

See vol. VI, Original ed. Bologna, 1768.

PART V.
MUSIC, INCLUDING OPERA.

Aikin, John: Essays on song writing ... London [?1772].

Four essays with illustrative anthologies appended: I, *On song-writing in general;* II, *On ballads and pastoral songs;* III, *On passionate and descriptive songs;* IV, *On ingenious and witty songs.* Other eds. 1714, 1777, 1810. See *Critical review* XXXIII, 182.

Alembert, Jean le Rond d': Elémens de musique théorique et practique, suivant les principes de M. Rameau ... Lyon ... 1762.

Also ed. 1779.

Alembert, Jean le Rond d': Sur la liberté de la musique. Paris ... 1760.

Algarotti, Count: Essay on opera ... [tr.]. Glasgow ... 1764.

Written 1755 and privately printed 1755. Also eds. 1762 and London, 1767. See *The lyric muse etc., a supplement* to Algarotti's *On opera.*

Analytical Review: VI, February, 1790, 132—133, Review of A general history of music from earliest ages to the present period, by Dr. Burney. Contains observations on music and poetry. See also VII, 33.

Annual Register: 1763, 192, A regular plan of music; 1769, 211, On modern music; 1772, 183, A censure of the present taste in music.

Antoniotto, Giorgio: L'Arte armonica, or A treatise on

composition of music, in three books ... London ...
1760.

For the most part a tchnical treatise on harmony, but the
Introduction and Bk. I, Chap. i, gives some general consideration to music as a fine art. See *Critical review* XI, 18.

[Armstrong, John] Launcelot Temple [pseud.] : Sketches,
London, 1748.

See essay on *Singing.*

Arteaga, S.: Le revoluzioni del teatro musicale Italiano,
Venizia, 1785 [2nd ed.].

See especially Chap. i, *Saggio analitico sulla natura del dramma
musicale,* etc. Also 1st. ed. Bologna, 1783—1788. See *Monthly
review* LXXVII, 545.

Avison, Charles: Essay on musical expression ... London,
1752.

See especially sections, *On the force and effect of music, On
the analogies between music and painting,* etc. 2nd ed. "with
alterations and large additions," London, 1753. 3rd ed., London,
1775. See also *Remarks on Mr. Avison's essay on musical expression* ... London, 1753, attributed to W. Hayes. See also
Avison's *A reply to the author of Remarks on the Essay on
musical expression,* London, 1752.

Bayly, Anselm: The alliance of musick, poetry and
oratory ... London ... 1789.

See especially pp. 79—320.

Bayly, Anselm: A practical treatise on singing and
playing ... London ... 1771.

See especially pp. 28—99 on singing.

Beattie, James: Essays on poetry and music as they
affect the mind ... Edinburgh ... 1776.

See especially Chap. vi on music.

Beattie, James: A letter to the Rev. Hugh Blair ... on

the improvement of psalmody in Scotland ... Edinburgh ... 1839.

Written and printed in 1778, but not published. It contains remarks on the relation of music and religion.

Bedford, A.: The great abuse of music ... London, 1711,

See especially Part II, Chap. i, containing some few æsthetic dicta.

Bee, The [ed. O. Goldsmith]: 1759, No. viii, 248, On opera in England.

Bonnot de Condillac, Abbé Etienne: Essay on the origin of human knowledge ... London ... 1756.

Tr. T. Nugent. See especially the section on music. French ed. 1746 and Amsterdam 1756.

Borghese, A. D. R.: A new and general system of music; or the art of music ... translated from the original Italian by John Gunn ... London ... 1740.

Bos, Abbé Jean Baptiste du: Critical reflections on poetry, painting and music ... London ... 1748 [tr. Thomas Nugent].

1st French ed. ? 1719; 7th French ed. 1770.

Brossard, Sebastian de: Dictionaire de musique, Amsterdam, 1703.

Contains a valuable bibliography. See *Monthly review* N. S., XXXVIII (1802) 215. 6th ed. Amsterdam, 1710. In English: *A musical dictionary*, tr. J. Grossineau, London, 1740.

Brown, John (not "Estimate" Brown): Letters upon the poetry and music of the Italian opera ... Edinburgh ... 1789.

Also ed. London, 1791.

Brown, Dr. John: History of the rise and progress of poetry through it's [*sic*] several species ... Newcastle, 1764.

Treats of melody, dance and poetry in the savage and civilized states and discusses their principles and history.

Brown, Dr. John ("Estimate"): A dissertation on the
rise, union, and power, the progressions, separations,
and corruptions, of poetry and music ... London ...
1763.

Tr. Ital. 1772. See *Some observations on Dr. Brown's disser-*
tation on the rise, union etc. of poetry and music, London,
1764. See *Remarks on Some observations on Dr. Brown's disser-*
tation ... London, 1764. See *Annual register*, 1763, 195: *Re-*
marks on our cathedral and parochial music (from Dr. Brown's
Dissertation on poetry and music).

[Browne, Richard]: A mechanical essay on singing, music
and dancing ... [London] 1727.

Originally published as *Medecina musica*.

Burney, Charles: General history of music from the
earliest ages to the present period ... London ...
1776—89.

See especially the *Preface* for æsthetic dicta. See *Analytical*
review VI, February, 1790. Ger. tr. 1781.

Burney, Charles: Present state of music in France and
Italy ... London ... 1771.

See especially the *Introduction*. See *Critical review* XXXVI, 34;
XXXVII, 77. 2nd ed. corrected, London, 1773.

Busby, Thomas: A complete dictionary of music to which
is prefixed a familiar introduction to the first principles of that science, 1786, and with additions,
1801.

[Chabanon, Michel Paul Guy de]: De la musique considérée elle-même, et dans ses rapports avec la
parole, les langues, la poésie et le théâtre ...
[2 vols.], Paris ... 1785.

See *Monthly review* LXXIII, 490.

[Chabanon, M. P. G. de]: Observations sur la musique,
et principalement sur la metaphysique de l'art ...
Paris ... 1779.

See *Monthly review* LXII, 541.

Chastellux, François Jean de: Essai sur l'union de la poésie et de la musique . . . La Haye . . . 1765.

Clarke, Jonas: The use and excellency of vocal music, in public worship. A sermon . . . Boston [Mass.], 1770.

Chiefly on the religious edification of music.

Corfe, Joseph: A treatise on singing . . . with some observations on vocal music . . . London [c. 1800].

See Monthly review XXXVI N. S., 148.

[Cooper, John Gilbert]: The power of harmony: a poem in two books . . . London . . . 1745.

See especially Book I. The harmony of music, poetry, and the imitative arts.

Critical review: XXXI, 458.

De la musique considérée elle-même, et dans ses rapports avec la parole, les langues, la poésie et le théâtre: See Chabanon, M. P. G. de.

Dennis, John: Essay on the operas, after the Italian manner . . . London . . . 1706.

Drake, N.: The gleaner . . . London . . . 1811.

See especially No. 168 On the powers of music.

Dyer, George: Poetics . . . London . . . 1812.

See especially the appended Disquisitions. Chap. xv.

Eastcott, Rev. Richard: Sketches of the origin, progress and effects of music, with an account of the ancient bards and minstrels . . . Bath . . . 1793.

See especially the chapters on music as an imitative art and on the utility of music. See Monthly review XIII N. S., 45. Also ed. London, 1793.

Essay toward the improvement of the musical arts, An: . . . Glasgow, 1798.

Essay upon tune, An: See Maxwell, John.

Essays, moral and literary: See Knox, V.

Euterpe, or remarks on the use and abuse of music as a part of modern education ... London ... [1778?].

See *Monthly review* LXI, 64.

Feyjoo [y Montenegro, Benito Geronimo]: Essays or discourses, selected from . . . translated from the Spanish by John Brett . . . London . . . 1780.

See especially II, 313, essays on church music and on the effects of music, and a comparison of the ancient with the modern. See *Monthly review* LVIII, 404.

Goldsmith, O.: See the Bee.

Grassineau, James: See Brossard, Sebastian de.

Grétry [André Ernest Modeste]: Mémoires, ou essais sur la musique . . . Paris, V. de la Rep.

See *Monthly review* XXIV N. S., 481.

Gunn, John: The art of playing the German flute . . . London . . . [1793].

See especially Chap. viii on musical expression. See also Borghese, A. D. R.

Hawkins, Sir John: A general history of the science and practice of music . . . London . . . 1776.

See especially the *Preliminary discourse*. Also eds. 1853, 1875.

Hayes, William: See Avison, C.

Hemsterhuis, M. F.: Œuvres philosophiques ... Paris ... 1792.

Holden, John: An essay toward a rational system of music . . . Glasgow . . . 1770.

See especially Chap. i. See *Critical review* XXXIII, 323.

Holder, William: Treatise on the natural grounds and principles of harmony . . . London . . . 1694.

Also ed. London, 1731, "corrected and revised."

Jackson, William: The four ages; together with essays on various subjects . . . London . . . 1798.

See especially p. 355, *On the joining of poetry and music;* p. 441, *On poetical and musical ear.* See *Critical review* XXII N. S., 262; *Monthly review* XXVI N. S., 190.

[Jackson, William]: Thirty letters on various subjects ... London . . . 1783.

See especially essays viii *On musical expression* and xvii *The passions not excited by music.* See *Monthly review* LXVIII, 391, and *Gentlemen's magazine* LIII, 332. 2nd ed., corrected, London, 1784; 3rd ed., with considerable additions, London, 1795.

Jackson, William: Observations on the present state of music in London, London, 1791.

See *Monthly review* VI N. S., 196.

Jacob, Hildebrand: Of the sister arts ... London ... 1734.

Jamard [T.]: Recherches sur la théorie de la musique, Paris, 1769.

Jones, William [of Nayland; not Sir William]: Physio- logical disquisitions; or discourses on the natural philosophy of the elements . . . London . . . 1781.

See especially Discourse vi, on sound and music.

[Jones, William, of Nayland]: A treatise on the art of music . . . Colchester . . . 1784.

See especially the *Introduction.* See *Monthly review* LXXV, 105 and 174.

Keeble, John: Theory of harmonics [applied especially to Greek music] . . . London . . . 1784.

See *Monthly review* LXXIII, 343 and 441.

King, M. P.: A general treatise on music . . . London . . . [1800].

See *Monthly review* XXXII N. S., 382.

[Knox, Vicesimus]: Essays, moral and literary, London . . . 1778.

See especially II, xxx, on music. 2nd ed. enlarged, 1779.

Kollmann, Augustus Friedric Christoph: An essay on musical harmony . . . London . . . 1796.

See especially *Introduction* on music as an art and its relation to language. See *Monthly review* XXI N. S., 27.

Kollman[n], Augustus Frederic Christopher: An essay on practical musical composition . . . London . . . 1799.

See *Critical review* XVIII N. S., 88; and XXVIII, 219. See also *Monthly review* XXXI N. S., 127.

Lampe, John Frederick: The art of music . . . London . . . 1740.

Locke, M.: See Salmon, Thomas.

Lover of church music, A: See Remarks upon church music.

Lyric muse revived in Europe, The, or a critical display of the opera in all its revolutions, London . . . 1768.

See especially the *Preface* which calls this work a "supplement" to Count Algarotti's *Essay.* See *Critical review* XXV, 457.

[Mainwaring, John]: Memoirs of the life of the late George Frederic Handel, to which is added a catalogue of his works, and observations upon them . . . London . . . 1760.

See especially the paragraphs of "the degrees of musical excellence" introducing the discussion of Handel's works. See *Critical review* XV, 212. Tr. Ger. 1761.

Malcolm, Alexander: A treatise of musick, speculative, practical and historical . . . Edinburgh . . . 1721.

2nd ed. "corrected and abridged," 1779.

Mason, William: Essays, historical and critical, on English church music . . . York . . . 1795.

See *Monthly review* XX N. S., 398. Essay ii had previously appeared as an introduction to *A copious collection of those portions of the psalms of David . . . published for the use of the church of York . . . York . . . 1782.*

Mattei, Saverio: Memore pere servire alla vita del Meta-
stasio . . . Colle, 1785.

See appended remarks on opera.

[Maxwell, John]: An essay upon tune, being an attempt
to free the scale of music, and the tune of instru-
ments from imperfections . . . Edinburgh . . . 1781.

See *Monthly review* LXV, 457.

Melody, the soul of music: An essay towards the improvement of the musical art . . . Glasgow . . . 1798.

See *Monthly review* XXVII N. S., 189.

Memoirs of the life of the late George Frederic Handel:
See Mainwaring, John.

Monthly review: LXXV, 105; VI N. S., 196; XII N. S.,
361, on music.

Morley, T.: Introduction to practical music . . . London,
1771 [reprint from 1597].

[? North, Francis, Lord Guilford]: A philosophical essay
of musick . . . London . . . 1677.

Observations sur la musique, et principalement sur la
metaphysique de l'art: See Chabanon, M. P. G. de.

Overend, Marmaduke: A brief account of, and an introduction to eight lectures in the science of music
. . . London . . . 1781.

See *Monthly review* LXVIII, 451.

Petit, J. C.: Apologie de l'excellence de la musique . . .
et une dissertation préliminaire et abregée sur les
moynes de perfectioner la musique et la faire fleurir
de plus en plus . . . Londres . . . [? 1740].

Philosophical essay of musick, A: See North, Francis.

Playford, John: An introduction to the skill of musick,
in three books . . . the twelfth edition . . . [London],
1694.

Also eds. 1658. 1660, 1662 etc.

Potter, John: Observations on the present state of music and musicians . . . London . . . 1762.

See *Critical review* XIV, 211.

Power of harmony, The: See Cooper, J. G.

Principles and power of harmony, The: See Stillingfleet, Benjamin.

Rameau [Jean Philippe]: Observations sur notre instinct pour la musique et sur son principe . . . Paris . . . 1754.

Remarks upon church music; to which are added several observations upon some of Mr. Handel's oratorios . . . by a lover of harmony . . . London . . . 1764.

See *Monthly review* XX, 86.

Rousseau, J[ean] J[acques]: A complete dictionary of music . . . translated . . . by William Waring, second edition, London, 1779.

See especially *sub imitation, music* and *opera*. See *Monthly review* LX, 122. 1st ed., Paris, 1768.

Rousseau, J. J.: Eloisa: or, a series of original letters . . . Dublin . . . 1761.

See especially letters xlvii, xlviii, lii, lxxxviii. 1st French ed., 1761, as *Lettres de deux amants*.

Rousseau [J. J.]: Letter . . . to M. D'Alembert . . . concerning the effects of theatrical entertainment on the manners of mankind . . . London, 1759.

See *Monthly review* XX, 115. See *Critical review* VII, 48. French ed. Amsterdam, 1758.

Rousseau, Jean Jacques: Lettre sur la musique française . . . [Paris], 1753.

2nd ed. 1753. Also much pamphlet discussion by D'Alembert and others.

Salmon, Thomas: An essay to the advancement of musick

by casting away the perplexity of different cliffs
. . . London . . . 1672.

See especially Chap. i on the advantage of music. See also
M. Locke's *Observations*, 1672, and his *Present practice of
musick*, 1673, in reply. See also Salmon's *A vindication of an
essay to the advancement of musick from Mr. Matthew Locke's
Observations . . . London . . . 1672.*

Salmon, Thomas: A proposal to perform musick in perfect mathematical proportions . . . London . . . 1688.

See especially chapter ii on *The principles of the present
practice.*

Smith, Robert: Harmonics, or the philosophy of musical
sounds . . . Cambridge . . . 1749.

See *Critical review* X, 249—56. 2nd ed., enlarged, Cambridge,
1759.

Smith, Robert: A postscript, to Dr. Smith's Harmonics,
upon the changeable harpsichord, London, 1778.

See *Critical review* XV, 159. Also in 2nd (augmented) edition
of *Harmonics* 1759—62.

Spectator, The: No. 5, March 6, 1711, On the absurdities
of the modern opera, attributed to Addison. No. 18,
March 21, 1711, History of the Italian opera, attributed to Addison. No. 29, April 3, 1711, Italian
recitative; absurdities of the opera dresses, attributed to Addison. No. 405, June 14, 1712, On
the improvement of sacred music, attributed to
Addison.

Stiles, Sir Francis Haskins Eyles: An explanation of the
modes in the antient Græcian music . . . Read at
several meetings of the Royal Society, London . . .
1761.

[Stillingfleet, Benjamin]: The principles and power of
harmony . . . London . . . 1771.

An adaptation of Tartini noted below. See *Critical review* XXXI,
458; XXXII, 15.

Tartini, Giuseppe: Trattato di musica secondo la vera
scienza dell'armonia [ed. D. A. Trento] . . . Padova
. . . 1754.

See also an Eglish adaptation by Stillingfleet, Benjamin.

Taylor, John: The music speech at the public commencement at Cambridge, July 6, 1730 . . . London . . .
1730.

Texier, Le: Idées sur l'opéra, London, 1790.

Also English tr. 1790.

Thirty letters: See Jackson, William.
Treatise on the art of music, A: See Jones, Wm.
Trydell, John: Two essays on the theory and practice
of music . . . Dublin . . . 1766.

See especially the *Preface.*

Turner, William: Sound anatomized in a philosophical
essay on musick . . . London . . . 1724.

3rd ed. ? 1740.

Twining, Thomas: Aristotle's Treatise on poetry translated with . . . two dissertations on poetical and
musical imitation . . . London . . . 1789.

See *Monthly review* IV N. S., 383; VII N. S., 121; XI N. S., 241.

Ville-sur-Illon, Bernard G. E. de la, Count de la Cepède:
La poétique de la musique . . . Paris . . . 1785.

See especially Book ii on theatrical music. See *Monthly review*
LXXII, 495. Also ed. 1798.

Vincent, William: Considerations on parochial music . . .
London . . . 1787.

An appendix to "Dr. Brown's Treatise on music." See *Advertisement.* See *Monthly review* LXXVIII, 250. 2nd ed. 1790.

Walker, Joseph C.: Historical memoirs of the Irish bards
. . . London . . . 1786.

See especially p. 65 on *The characteristic features and genera
of the Irish music.*

Webb [Daniel]: Observations on the correspondence between poetry and music . . . London . . . 1769.

See *Critical review* XXVIII, 107.

West, Benjamin: Sacra concerto: or the voice of melody. Containing an introduction to the gounds of music . . .

See *Critical review* IX, 77. I have been unable to examine a copy of this work.

APPENDIX.

SOME RECENT COMMENT ON EIGHTEENTH CENTURY ÆSTHETICS.

Abbey, C. A.: The English church and its bishops, London, 1887.

Abercrombie, Lascelles: An essay toward theory of art, London, 1922.

Abercrombie, Lascelles: The idea of great poetry, London, 1925.

Abercrombie, Lascelles: Romanticism, London, 1926.

Alden, R. M.: The romantic defence of poetry. In Schelling anniversary papers, New York, 1923.

Amos, Flora Ross: Early theories of translation, New York, 1920.

Armstrong, Sir Walter: Gainsborough, London, 1899.

Armstrong, Sir Walter: Sir Joshua Reynolds, New York, 1900.

Aydelotte, Frank: The Oxford stamp and other essays, New York, 1917.

> See especially p. 177, on Blair's, Cämpbell's, and Whateley's theories of thetoric.

Babbitt, Irving: Dr. Johnson and imagination, Southw. rev. XIII, 25.

Babbitt, Irving: The new Laokoon, New York, 1900.

Babbitt, Irving: Rousseau and romanticism, Boston, 1919.

Bailey, J. C.: Studies in some famous letters, London, 1899.

Bailey, M.: Boswell as essayist, Jour. Eng. Ger. phil., XXII, 412.

Barrett, W. A.: English church composers, New York and London, 1882.

Bateman, C. T.: William Gilpin, artist and author. In Pap. Man. lit. club, XIX, 301.

Beatty, A.: William Wordsworth: his doctrine and art in their historical relations, Madison, Wis. 1922. In Univ. of Wis. stud. in lang. and lit., No. 17.

Beers, Henry A.: A history of English romanticism in the eighteenth century, New York, 1898.

Benson, F. L.: The English hymn, London, 1915.

Bergmann, Ernst: Geschichte der Ästhetik und Kunstphilosophie, Leipzig, 1914.

Bernbaum, E.: Drama of Sensibility, Boston and London, 1915.

Binyon, L.: English poetry in its relation to painting and the other arts, 1918. In Proc. Brit. acad., 1921, 381.

Black, J. B.: The art of history: a study of four great historians of the 18th century, New York, 1926.

Bloomfield, R.: Short history of gothic, London, 1900.

Bosanquet, B.: Hegel's philosophy of fine art, London, 1886.

Bosanquet, B.: History of æsthetics, New York, 1917.

Bray, J. W.: History of English critical terms, Boston, 1898.

Bredvold, L. I.: Introduction to Selected poems of Alexander Pope, New York, 1926.

Brooke, S. A.: Naturalism in English poetry, New York, 1920.

Brown, J. E.: The critical opinions of Samuel Johnson, Princeton, 1926.

Brownfield, L. B.: A study in the thought of Addison, Johnson, and Burke, Indiana Univ. diss. Privately printed, 1918.

Burchardt, C.: English humor og vidd under dronning Annas regjering, Edda, 22, 3, pp. 54—84.

Burd, H. A.: The golden age in 18th century poetry, Sew. rev., XXIII, 172.

Burnet, John: Treatise on painting, 1829.

Bywater, I.: Aristotle on the art of poetry, London, 1902.

Campbell, O. J., and Menschke, P.: 'Guilt and sorrow': a study in the genesis of Wordsworth's æsthetic. Mod. phil., XXIII, 293.

Cozamian, Louis: History of English literature, London, 1926—27; Vol. II, Modern times.

Chesneau, E.: English school of painting, London, 1891.

Clark, Alexander F. B.: Boileau and the French classical critics in England 1660—1830, Paris, 1925.

Clark, H. H.: A study of melancholy in Edward Young, Mod. lang. notes, XXXIX, 129 and 193.

Clapp, J. M.: An eighteenth century attempt at a critical view of the novel, Pub. mod. lang. assoc., XXV, 60.

Clément, F.: Histoire générale de la musique religeuse, Paris, 1878.

Conant, M. P.: The oriental tale in England in the eighteenth century, New York, 1908.

Collins, J. C.: Studies in poetry and criticism, London, 1905, p. 215.

Cowl, R. P.: The theory of poetry in England: its development in doctrine and ideas from the sixteenth to the nineteenth century, London, 1914.

Crane, R. S.: Imitation of Spenser and Milton in the early eighteenth century: a new document, Stud. in phil., XV, 195.

Creighton, J. E.: 18th and 19th century modes of thought, Philos. rev., XXXV, 1.

Croce, B.: Philosophy of Giambattista Vico, tr. R. G. Collingwood. New York, 1913.

Damon, Samuel Foster: William Blake: his philosophy and symbols, Boston, 1924.

Dibelius, W.: Englische Romankunst, Berlin, 1910.

Dickenson, Edward: Music in the history of the western church, New York, 1903.

Dixon, W. M.: English epic and heroic poetry, New York, 1912.

Dobrée, Bonamy: Restoration comedy, 1660—1720, Oxford, 1924.

Doughty, O.: The English lyric in the age of reason, London, 1922.

Drake, Maurice: A history of English glass painting, London, 1912.

Draper, J. W.: Aristotelian μίμησις in eighteenth century England, Pub. mod. lang. assoc., XXXVI, 372.

Draper, J. W.: The summa of romanticism, The colonnade (1922), XIV, 257.

Draper, J. W.: The theory of translation in the eighteenth century, Neophilologus VI, 244.

Draper, J. W.: William Mason, a study in eighteenth century culture, New York, 1924.

Durham, W. H.: Critical essays of the 18th century, New Haven, 1915.

Dutton, G. B.: Thomas Rymer, Pub. mod. lang. assoc., XXIX, 186.

Eastlake, Sir Charles: The gothic revival, London, 1872.

Egan, Rose Frances: The genesis of the theory of art for art's sake in Germany and England. Smith College studies, II, No. 4, July 1921, Northampton, Mass., U. S. A.

Elton, O.: Reason and enthusiasm in the eighteenth century, Essays and studies, X, 122.

Flasdieck, H. M.: Introduction to John Brown's Dissertation on poetry and music (1764), Halle, 1924.

Folkierski, W.: Entre le classicisme et le romantisme: étude sur l'esthétique et les esthéticiens du XVIII siècle. Cracow and Paris, 1925.

Fournier-Pargoire, Jeanne: L'esprit classique en Angleterre, Revue hebdomadaire III, 18.

Frye, H.: Drayden and the critical canons of the eighteenth century, Lincoln, Neb., U. S. A., 1907.

Gayley, C. M., and Scott, F. N.: Guide to the literature of æsthetic. Berkeley [Cal.], 1890.

Gillman, F. J.: Evolution of the English hymn, London, 1927.

Gomme, G. L.: The gentleman's magazine library, Boston, n. d.

Göricke, Walter: Das Bildungsideal bei Addison und Steele, Bonn, 1921.

Gothein, Marie Luise: Geschichte der Gartenkunst, Jena, 1914. (English tr. by W. P. Wright, London, 1928.)

Greenbie, Mrs. M. L.: Wordsworth's theory of poetic diction, New Haven, 1917.

Grierson, H. J. C.: Classical and romantic, Cambridge [England], 1923.

Guedalla, Philip: Mr. Burke and the grand manner, Nation-Athenaeum, 1926, XXXVIII, 18, 19, 610, 644.

Gysin, A.: Die Gesellschaft Englands in der Hälfte des 18. Jahrhunderts nach der Literatur der Zeit (1760 bis 1800), Marburg, 1914.

Hamelius, Paul: Die Kritik in der eng. Literatur des 17. und 18. Jahrhunderts, Bruxelles, 1897.

Hansen, A.: Addison som litterær kritiker, Copenhagen, 1883.

Havens, R. D.: The influence of Milton in English poetry. Cambridge [Mass.], 1922.

See especially XIX on the sonnet.

Havens, R. D.: The poetic diction of the English classicists, Kittredge anniv. papers, New York, 1913. •

Hecht, Hans: Introduction to Daniel Webb's Remarks on the beauties of poetry (1762), Hamburg, 1920.

Herrick, M. T.: Joseph Trapp and the Aristotelian "Catharsis," Mod. lang. notes, XLI, 158.

Herrick, M. T.: The Poetics of Aristotle in England. Cornell Studies XVII, New Haven [Conn.], 1930.

Herman, Conrad: Die Ästhetik in ihrer Geschichte und als wissenschaftliches System, Leipzig, 1876.

Houston, P. H.: Dr. Johnson, a study in eighteenth century humanism, Cambridge [Mass.], 1923.

Howard, W. G.: Burke among the forerunners of Lessing. Pub. mod. lang. assoc., XXII, 608.

Howard, W. G.: Good taste and conscience. Pub. mod. lang. assoc., XXV, 486.

Howard, W. G.: Ut pictura poesis. In Pub. mod. lang. assoc., XXIV, 40.

Howes, R. F.: Coleridge and rhetoric. Quart. jour. of speech educ., XII, 145.

Hussey, Christopher: The picturesque, studies in a point of view, London and New York [1927].

Jones, R. F.: Eclogue types in English poetry of the eighteenth century, Jour. Eng. Ger. phil., XXIV, 33.

Kaufman, Paul: Heralds of original genius. In Essays in memory of Barrett Wendell, Cambridge [Mass.], 1926.

Kaufman, Paul: John Foster's pioneer interpretation of the romantic. Mod. lang. notes, XXXVIII, 1.

Ker, W. P.: On the value of the terms 'classical' and 'romantic' as applied to literature. In Collected esays, London, 1925.

Ker, W. P.: Romantic fallacies. In the Art of poetry, Oxford, 1923.

Knipe, J. W.: The development of literary criticism in England. In Trans. of Roy. soc. of lit., XIX, 223, Sec. Ser.

Krehbiel, H. E.: Music and manners in the classical period, New York, 1898.

Krehbiel, H. R.: See Sturgis, R.

Laurencie, L. de la: Lully, Paris, 1911.

Lemonnier, Henri: La mégalomanie dans l'architecture (L'Art moderne, 1500—1800), Paris, 1912.

Lilly, Marie L.: The georgic, Baltimore, 1917.

Lloyd, Mary: Elegies, ancient and modern, Trenton [N. J.], 1903.

Lombard, A.: L'abbé du Bos, initiateur de la pensée moderne, Paris, 1913.

Longueil, A. E.: The word 'gothic' in eighteenth century criticism. Mod. lang. notes, XXXVIII, 453.

Loudon, John Claudius: An encyclopaedia of gardening, London, 1822.

> See especially the bibliography. Also ed. 1835; new ed. corrected, 1850.

Lounsbury, T. R.: Shakespeare and Voltaire, New York, 1902.

Lounsbury, T. R.: Shakespeare as a dramatic artist, New York, 1901.

> See especially IX.

Lounsbury, T. R.: The text of Shakespeare: its history and publication, including the editions of Theobald and Pope, New York, 1906.

Lovejoy, A. O.: Nature as an æsthetic norm, Mod. lang. notes, XLII, 444.

Lovejoy, A. O.: On the discrimination of romanticisms, Pub. mod. lang. assoc., XXXIX, 229.

Lovejoy, A. O.: Optimism and romanticism. Pub. mod. assoc., XLII, 921.

Lovejoy, A. O.: Schiller and the genesis of romanticism. Mod. lang. notes, XXXV, 1, 136.

Maar, Harko De: A history of modern English romanticism, Vol. I, Oxford, 1924.

McCutcheon, R. P.: Beginning of book-reviewing, Pub. mod. lang. assoc., XXXVI, 9.

McKillop, A. D.: The romanticism of William Collins, Stud. in phil., XX, 1.

Manwaring: The Italian landscape in eighteenth century England, New York, 1925.

Mason, D. G.: The art of music, New York, 1915—17.

Mead, W. E.: The versification of Pope in relation to the seventeenth century, Leipzig, 1889.

Meier-Gräfe, Julius: The development of modern art, New York, 1908.

Menschke, P.: See Campbell, O. J.

Millar, J. H.: Scottish prose in the seventeenth and eighteenth centuries, Glasgow, 1913.

Milsand, J.: L'esthétique anglaise, étude sur M. John Ruskin, Paris, 1864.

See especially the *Introduction*.

Mirabent y Vilaplana, Francisco: La estética inglesa del siglo XVIII, Barcelona, 1927.

Monkhouse, C.: Early English water color painters, London, 1890.

Moore, C. A.: Shaftesbury and the ethical poets of England, Pub. mod. lang. assoc., XXXI, 264.

More, P. E.: The drift of romanticism, London, 1913.

Morgan, C. E.: The rise of the novel of manners 1660—1740, New York, 1911.

Morley, Edith J.: Introduction to Edward Young's Conjectures on original composition, Manchester, 1918.

Mornet, Daniel: La Question des Régles au XVIIIe siécle. In Rev. d'hist. lit. de la France, XXI, 241, 595.

Mornet, Daniel: Le romantisme en France, Paris, 1912.

Murry, J. M.: Discoveries, London, 1924.

See esepcially 153, *English poetry of the 18th century*.

Muther, Richard: History of modern painting, London, 1907.

Muther, Richard: History of painting, New York, 1907.

Nolen, John, editor: The art of landscape gardening, by Humphry Repton, Boston, 1907.

Omond, T. S.: English metrists of the eighteenth and nineteenth centuries, London, 1907.

Partridge, Eric: The 1762 efflorescence of poetics. Stud. in phil., XXV, 27.

Partridge, Eric: Vicesimus Knox: his Essays moral and literary, Paris, 1926.

Pierce, Frederick E.: Romanticism and other isms, Jour. Eng. Ger. phil., XXVI, 451.

Plessow, M.: Geschichte der Fabeldichtung in England bis zu John Gay 1726, Berlin, 1906.

Pons, E.: Le 'voyage', genre litteraire au XVIIIe siècle, Strasbourg, 1926.

Pottle, F. A. and others: Burkes On the sublime. N. and Q. Jan. 31, 1925, CXLVIII, 80; Feb. 21, 1925, CXLVIII, 140.

Powell, A. E. [Mrs. E. P. Dodds]: The romantic theory of poetry, New York, 1926.

Prinsen, J.: De roman in de 18e eeuw in West-Europa, Groningen, 1925.

Prumières, H.: Lully, Paris [1909?].

Quayle, Thomas: Poetic diction: A study of eighteenth century verse, London, 1924.

Quigley, Hugh: Italy and the rise of a new school of criticism in the eighteenth century, Perth, 1924.

Railo, E.: The haunted castle: a study of the elements of English romanticism, London, 1927.

Rand, B.: Second characters, or the language of forms, by the Earl of Shaftesbury, Cambridge [England], 1919.

Raysor, T. M.: The downfall of the three unities, Mod. lang. notes, XLII, 1.

Raysor, T. M.: Unpublished fragments on æsthetics by T. S. Coleridge, Stud. in phil., XXII, 529.

Read, Herbert: Reason and romanticism. In Essays in literary criticism, London, 1926.

Redin, Mats: Word order in English verse from Pope to Sassoon, Uppsala, 1927.

Reynaud, Louis: Le romantisme, ses origines anglo-germaniques. Influences étrangères et traditions nationales, Paris, 1926.

Reynolds, Myra: Nature in poetry between Pope and Wordsworth, Chicago, 1896.

Rhys, E.: English lyric poetry, New York, 1913.

Riat, G.: L'art des jardins, Paris, 1900.

Richardson, C. F.: A study of English rhyme, Hanover [N. H.], 1909.

Riemann, H.: Die Elemente der musikalischen Ästhetik, Berlin, 1900.

Rinaker, C.: Thomas Warton and the historical method in criticism, Pub. mod. lang. assoc., XXX, 79.

Robertson, J. G.: Studies in the genesis of the romantic theory in the eighteenth century. Cambridge [England], 1923.

R[obertson], J. G.: Review of Flasdeick's ed. of Brown's Dissertation, Mod. lang. rev., XXI, 108.

Roget, J. L.: Old water color society, London, 1891.

Rolland, R.: Handel, New York, 1916.

Rosenberg, Alfred: Longinus in England bis zum Ende des 18. Jahrhunderts, Weimar, 1917.

Roscoe, E. S.: The English scene in the eighteenth century, New York, 1913.

Routh, J.: The rise of classical English criticism, New Orleans [? 1915].

Saintsbury, George: Historical manual of English prosody, New York, 1910.

Salt, L. G.: English heroic poetry, New York, 1913.

Sandby, W.: Royal academy of arts, London, 1862.

Saudé, E.: Die Grundlagen der literarischen Kritik bei Joseph Addison, Berlin, 1908.

Schasler, Max.: Kritische Geschichte der Ästhetik, Berlin, 1872.

Schlosser, J.: Die Kunstliteratur, Wien, 1924.

Schöffler, H.: Protestantismus und Literatur, Leipzig, 1922.

Sedding, J. D.: Gardencraft, old and new, New York, 1902.

Seiberth, Philipp: Romanticism, Germanic rev. I, 336.
Seillière, E.: Mal romantique, Paris, 1908.
Sherman, L. A.: Analytics of literature, Boston, 1893.
Sieveking, A. F.: The paise of gardens, London, 1899.
Smith, David Nicol: Shakespeare in the eighteenth century, Oxford, 1928.
Smith, M. E.: The fable in English criticism, Mod. lang. notes, XXXII, 466.
Snell, A. L. F.: An objective study of syllabic quantity in English verse, Pub. mod. lang. assoc., XXXIV, 416.
Spingarn, F. E.: Critical essays of the seventeenth century, Oxford, 1908.

See especially the *Introduction*.

Stein, K. H.: Die Entstehung der neueren Ästhetik, Stuttgart, 1886.
Steinke, M. W.: Edward Young's Conjectures on original composition, in England and Germany, New York, 1917.
Stokoe, F. W.: German influence in the English romantic period 1788—1818, Cambridge [England], 1926.
Sturgis, R., and Krehbiel, H.: Annotated bibliography of fine art and music, Boston, 1897.
Taylor, H. W.: Realism and the romantic spirit, Sewanee rev. XXXV, 336.
Texte, Joseph: J. J. Rousseau et les origines du cosmopolitanisme littéraire, Paris, 1895.
Thompson, E. N. S.: Discourses of Sir Joshua Reynolds, Pub. mod. lang. assoc., XXXII, 339.
Tieje, A. J.: The theory of characterization in prose fiction prior to 1740, Minneapolis [Minn.], 1916.
Tinker, C. B.: Nature's simple plan, Princeton [N. J.], 1922.
Turner, F. McD. C.: The development of irony in English literature, Cambridge [England], 1926.

Van Bever, A.: Les poètes du terroir du XVe siècle au XXe siècle, Paris, 1909.

Van Tieghem, Paul: Le mouvement romantique, Paris, 1923.

Van Tieghem, Paul: La notion de vraie poésie dans le préromanticisme européen. Rev. de la litt. comp., I, 215.

Van Tieghem, Paul: Le préromantisme: étude d'histoire littéraire européenne, Paris, 1924.

Vitry, Paul: C. A. Dufresnoy pictoris poemate quod "De arte graphica" inscribitur, Paris, 1901.

Walker, Hugh: English satire, London, 1925.

Walter, U.: Boileaus Wirkung auf seine englischen Zeitgenossen, Straßburg, 1913.

Waterhouse, Francis A.: Romantic 'Originality,' Sewanee rev. XXXIV, 40.

Whitney, Lois: English primitivistic theories of epic origins, Mod. phil., XXI, 337.

Wichelns, H. A.: Burke's Essay on the sublime and its reviewers, Jour. Eng. Ger. phil., XXI, 645.

Wilde, N.: The development of Coleridge's thought. Philos. rev. XXVIII, 147.

Williams, H.: Two centuries of the English novel, London, 1911.

Wood, Sir Henry Trueman: A history of the Royal society of arts, London, 1913.

Wood, P. S.: Nature elements in English neo-classicism, Mod. phil., XXIV, 201.